The A

How Managers Can Get Great Results from Good Ideas

By Jon Dario

The Amazing Link
How Managers Can Get
Great Results from Good Ideas

© 2020 by Jon Dario

All rights reserved. This book or any portion thereof may not be reproduced or used in any manner whatsoever without the express written permission of the publisher except for the use of brief quotations in a book review.

ISBN-13: 9781657811393

Contents

Prologue   The Amazing Link to a Championship

Chapter 1   Execution—The Amazing Link
Chapter 2   The Power of Positive Relationships
Chapter 3   Communicate
Chapter 4   Motivate
Chapter 5   Follow Up
Chapter 6   Grow Talent
Chapter 7   Building & Sustaining an Execution Culture

Appendix I   Performance Planning Process
Appendix II   Management Behaviors That Drive Execution
Appendix III   Execution Problems Diagnostic Tool

Acknowledgments
About the Author
Resources

Prologue—The Amazing Link to a Super Bowl Championship

The date is February 4, 2018, and the location is US Bank Stadium in Minneapolis, Minnesota. The Philadelphia Eagles are playing the New England Patriots in Super Bowl LII, the fifty-second edition of the National Football League's championship game. The Patriots have become one of the greatest dynasties in NFL history, having won two of the last three Super Bowls and gone to the Conference Championship game seven seasons in a row. The Eagles have never won a Super Bowl, and they have failed to advance beyond the first round of the playoffs for the last three seasons. Needless to say, the Patriots are favored to win.

Yet, midway through the second quarter, the Eagles are leading by a score of fifteen to six. And they are driving to score again and add to their lead. But a pass from Eagle quarterback Nick Foles is intercepted, and the Patriots march the other way down the field. Seven plays later, they score a touchdown, and the Philadelphia lead is cut to just three points. Football fans have seen this from the New England team time and again. The floodgates are now open, and fortune is on the side of the merciless Patriots. It's only a matter of time before they will pull ahead and start cruising to their third championship in four years.

But then a flicker of hope for Eagle fans appears! After the ensuing kickoff, Foles connects on a fifty-five-yard pass play, and the Eagles have the ball at the Patriots' eight-yard line with a first down and goal to go. They pick up six yards on first down but can only gain one more yard on second down. Third down is an incomplete pass, so the Eagles are facing fourth down at the Patriots' one-yard line. The flicker of hope is dimming. And there are just thirty-eight seconds left in the second quarter. The Patriots will receive the kickoff to start the second half, so if the Eagles don't score on this last opportunity before halftime, chances are good they will quickly fall behind at the start of the third quarter and never get another chance to catch up. The only question is whether they take the three points that would come with a field goal attempt, a virtual guarantee from this spot on the field, or risk going for a six-point touchdown. The risk is especially apparent given the last two unsuccessful plays. The Eagles call time-out to talk it over with head coach Doug Pederson.

The Eagles return from the time-out and line up as if they are going for the touchdown. The entire stadium and 103 million television viewers wait for the handoff that will send an Eagles running back crashing into the line of Patriot defenders. The winner of this battle will have all-important momentum behind them for the second half of the game, and that will be a deciding factor in the outcome. But then a surprise! The Eagles snap the ball directly to running back Corey Clement, and, as he runs to the left, he pitches it back to tight end Trey Burton. Burton throws the ball forward to quarterback Nick Foles, who has snuck out to the right side of the end zone and is unguarded. Foles catches the touchdown pass, the Eagles successfully kick the extra point after the touchdown, and they go into the locker room with a twenty-two to twelve lead at halftime. They go on to win the game and earn the first Super Bowl Championship in team history.

After the game, Coach Pederson was widely given credit for making one of the gutsiest play calls in Super Bowl history and, in doing so, giving the Eagles the energy and momentum they needed to win the game. But was the play really so creative that the idea of this play should get that much credit? In a twist of irony, the Patriots had attempted a nearly identical play less than twelve minutes earlier in the game. On third down with the ball on Philadelphia's thirty-five-yard line, New England wide receiver Danny Amendola threw a pass to quarterback Tom Brady, who was wide open on the right side of the field (sound familiar?). But the ball slipped through Brady's hands and fell incomplete. If Brady had caught the pass, he had room to run, and even if he didn't score, he would have put the Patriots into perfect position to score soon afterward. As it happened, on the next play, fourth down, the Patriots threw another incomplete pass and turned the ball over on downs. So the Eagles were actually the second team to try that same trick play in the game. The difference was that they executed it successfully while the Patriots did not.

The lesson of this story is that good ideas are only part of the process of achieving great results. The other necessary component is execution. Without execution, good ideas remain just that—ideas. Execution is the amazing link that turns ideas into results. This book is about the critical role that managers play in getting teams to execute successfully. As defined by Merriam-Webster "execute" means to carry out fully or to put completely in effect. Teams at work are asked to complete tasks, perform services, and meet ongoing performance standards. As we will discuss later in the book, successful execution means both complete and consistent performance of the behaviors required to perform the tasks, services, and performance standards. It is the performance of these on-the-job expectations rather than the idea of them that delivers results for a business.

We will explore the four most important behaviors that frontline managers use to generate consistent and complete execution. And, for each of those behaviors, we will discuss tools and models that can help new and experienced managers improve their ability to drive higher levels of execution from their teams.

This book is meant for three groups of people.

It is ideal for frontline managers who are primarily responsible for driving execution by the employees who are the face of the business and are directly in contact with customers. From this book, frontline managers will learn fundamental skills that will help them maximize effectiveness in delivering consistent execution and therefore delivering consistent results.

It is ideal for managers of frontline managers, meaning people with titles like district manager, area manager, and market manager. Managers of frontline managers will receive a road map for developing the skills and effectiveness of the people they directly supervise.

It is ideal for senior executives who decide on the strategies that must be executed at the front lines. Senior executives will see in this book the foundation of a training and development program that will increase the probability their frontline managers will drive more consistent execution.

Much of the book is written from the perspective of retail management. Not only is retail the foundation of my career, it is, in my opinion, the most complex environment in which to manage. Anybody who can successfully apply the concepts in this book in a retail setting can also do so in a less stressful, less dynamic setting.

Let's get started on the journey that will help you and your team turn good ideas into great results! For those of you who are listening to this as an audio book, or if you want full size versions of the tools and models you see in the paperback version, you can download every chart and tool we will discuss throughout the book from my website. You may find them at

http://www.RetailManagementFormula.com/TAL-downloads.

Chapter 1: Execution—The Amazing Link

Businesses are chock full of leaders who have ideas for how they can get better results. In fact, every business has somebody at the top who thinks they know how to achieve great results. The larger the business, the more leaders with ideas. So why doesn't every business end up with great results? The answer is simple: execution. Execution is the amazing link that turns good ideas into great results. Consider the image below.

Figure 1.1: The Execution Link

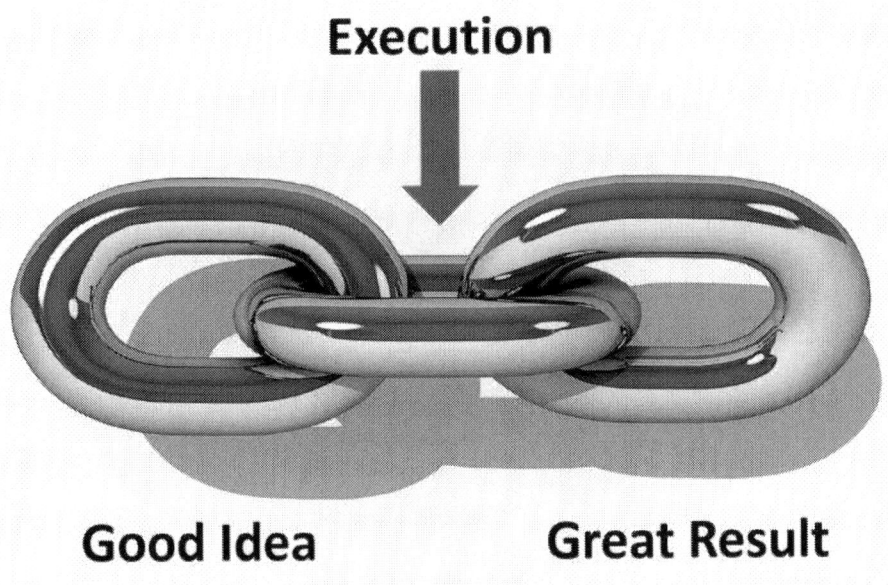

Ideas don't magically turn into great results all by themselves. Somebody must do something with each and every idea before great results can happen. For example, it's a good idea to exercise every day. Great results like losing weight and achieving a healthy heart don't happen just because you think about exercising; they happen when you execute the idea and actually do the exercise. It's a good idea to pay your bills on time. Great results like a strong credit rating and lower interest rates don't happen just because you think about paying your bills on time; they happen when you execute the idea and actually do pay your bills by the time they are due. In business, it's a good idea to treat customers well. Great results like customer loyalty and positive referral of more customers don't happen just because you think about treating people well; they happen when you execute the idea and actually do treat people well.

Perhaps the point is incredibly obvious. But the visual image of "execution" as the link between good ideas and great results is meant to shine a bright spotlight on the critical role that execution plays. This book is all about helping you leverage that link as a manager. We will explore the core concepts that are at the heart of execution, and we will discuss the behaviors that are most important for execution. But before we get too deep into execution, let's cover a few preliminary points.

I must acknowledge that great results can happen accidentally. An individual can have the idea that daily exercise will help with weight loss, fail to exercise at all, and still lose lots of weight by not eating as many calories. The intended result was achieved without execution, at least without execution of the original idea. In reality, a completely different idea was executed, whether intentionally or not. Execution of that different idea drove the result, and the result just happened to be the same as the originally intended result. For our purpose as managers, we're not interested in accidental results. We are interested in turning our ideas, or those of our coworkers, into great results. And that means we must execute those ideas.

So far, I have talked about ideas as if all ideas are good. That can't possibly be true, can it? Don't some ideas fail to turn into great results because the idea itself was bad? For example, what if somebody thought it would be a good idea to treat customers badly? That's certainly not an idea that could generate great results, is it?

Have you ever eaten at the restaurant named Dick's Last Resort? This establishment purposely hires obnoxious servers and then trains them to insult customers and treat customers badly. The chain has successful locations in thirteen cities and has become a tourist destination. Ironically, the founder originally had a fine dining restaurant that failed. And now he's built a very successful business that's based on the concept of treating customers poorly.

Why does this seemingly bad idea work out well? That's right—it works because of the way it is executed. One of the taglines on their website is "Putting the *F U* in fun." The bad treatment is all in the name of good fun, and the staff executes within that context.

Okay, now that I have you wanting to prove me wrong by thinking of other ideas that have absolutely no chance of turning into great results, I'll admit that there is indeed such a thing as a bad idea. To explain, allow me to tell a story.

I worked at a clothing retailer around the time that stores were beginning to install traffic counters on the doors. They were simple devices that emitted an infrared light beam that stretched across the store entrance threshold. Whenever a customer walked through the entrance, the beam was broken, and the traffic counter registered a customer walk-in. One of the most interesting calculations that could be made from the traffic counter data was conversion rate, or the percentage of customer walk-ins that resulted in a purchase in the store. Theoretically, the conversion percentage was a measure of how well the store did its job in selling to the customers who entered. Present the merchandise attractively, and more customers will buy. Provide great service, and more customers will buy. Effectively sign all of the best deals, and more customers will buy. So far, it makes sense, right?

Well, the company decided to benchmark performance standards based on the stores that had the highest conversion rates. The logic was if one store can convince 45 percent of walk-in customers to make a purchase, then every store should be able to do the same. They created a scorecard system that ranked store managers and district managers based on conversion rate, and they tied bonuses and performance appraisals to the rankings. The underlying idea was to get all stores operating at the same high level, and that would drive spectacular increases in revenue.

It sounded like a really good idea, except it was not executable. There were real differences among the stores that prevented that idea from being realistically achievable. Some stores were "destination" stores in drive-up strip centers, and others were in busy shopping malls where a large number of customers were simply wandering the mall for entertainment. Some stores were adjacent to busy restaurants where people used a store walk-through to kill time while waiting for their table. Some stores were used as a pass-through entrance to the mall from the parking lot. So the difference between a 15 percent conversion rate store and a 45 percent conversion rate store wasn't simply about the store's skill and effort in selling to customers. The idea of getting the 15 percent conversion rate store to become a 45 percent conversion rate store just wasn't executable.

So again, I admit there are bad ideas. Bad ideas are those that are unable to be executed. Going back to the idea of building a business on the concept of treating customers badly, Dick's Last Resort found a way to execute the idea successfully. That makes it a good idea. And no matter how good any other idea sounds, it's not really a good idea unless it can be successfully executed. It would be fantastic if consumers shopping for clothing online could immediately, while they are on their computer or mobile device, receive a sample to try on. But, as of the time of this writing, that's not possible, so it's a bad idea. The minute somebody finds a way to make it possible, it will become a good idea. Then the good idea can turn into great results when somebody actually executes it.

Now that we've covered the "idea" part of the equation, let's turn our attention back to execution. I'll start with a discussion of the connection between actions and results.

I like to use a special tool to show the relationship between actions, or behaviors, and results. I call it the "Behaviors–Results Grid." The premise of this grid is that while behaviors do drive results, the two are not always visibly aligned. Common sense says that good behaviors will create good results, and bad behaviors will create bad results. At least that's what my parents always told me. Then I'd watch people do bad things and get good results, and I would question why I was such a fool for feeling the pressure to be a good guy.

I'm sure you, too, deal with it every day. You're commuting to work in stop-and-go traffic, and you see the one driver who thinks he is more important than everybody else cruise up the shoulder of the road past the stopped cars and cut in at the last second. That was a bad behavior. But what happens to him? Does he get pulled over by the police? Does his brand-new Mercedes get damaged as he cuts in front of the delivery truck? Do his tires get slashed by the debris in the shoulder? No, none of those bad results happen. What really happens is that he saves ten minutes on his commute and makes everybody else wait just a little bit longer. Okay, maybe this example is particularly poignant for those of you who live in my home state of New Jersey, but you get the idea. The self-important driver gets a good result for himself despite his bad behavior. So what does this say about the relationship between behaviors and results? Let's explore the question with Figure 1.2 below.

Figure 1.2: The Behaviors–Results Grid

| | | **Behaviors** ||
		Bad	Good
Results	Good	Success by accident or due to external factors; better results are left on the table	Ideal situation
	Bad	Unacceptable situation	May need more time; results are better than they would otherwise be without the good behaviors

In the Behaviors–Results Grid, the two components are set off against each other with behaviors across the top of the grid and results down the side of the grid. Each component is split into two sections: good and bad. That creates a four-box grid that shows all of the possible combinations of good and bad behaviors and good and bad results.

The top right box in the grid represents good behaviors and good results. This is the relationship we hope and expect to see. It's an ideal situation; execute good behaviors, and receive good results. Going back to an earlier example, it's the situation where you eat less calories and exercise more frequently, and you lose weight.

The bottom left box in the grid represents the opposite scenario, that of bad behaviors and bad results. Again, this is a relationship we expect to see. Consume more calories and exercise less frequently, and you expect the negative result (assuming you wanted to lose weight, that is). When it comes to performance on the job, this is an unacceptable situation since the bad result is presumably a function of poor execution.

These first two boxes are easy to identify and explain. If you observe good behaviors that lead to good results, the connection seems obvious. If you observe bad behaviors that lead to bad results, that connection also seems obvious. The other two boxes are more complicated, and they are often the source of traps for unwitting managers.

The top left box in the grid is like our self-important driver passing everybody by using the shoulder. This box represents situations where bad behaviors produce good results. These are tricky situations for managers. When we see good results, we tend to think, "That person must be doing something right." But the Behaviors–Results Grid tells us that the two things are not necessarily connected so directly. Several things are possible within this box on the grid, including the following:

- The good result is random luck that will not be repeated consistently.
- The good result is driven by some external factor that is more powerful than the bad behavior that was observed.
- The bad behavior is driving some other bad result, even if the observed result is good.

Going back to our selfish driver example, perhaps he didn't get pulled over by the police this time, but the more often he drives down the shoulder, the greater his chance of getting caught and receiving a ticket. Or perhaps the extreme anxiety that compels him to be such an obnoxious driver is causing him health problems that will take years off of his hectic life. I wonder if he'd make the same behavioral choice if that bad result were as obvious and visible as the short-term good result of saving a few minutes of commute time.

When it comes to management, there is an important fact about situations where good results are obtained despite bad behaviors. That fact is that better results are left on the table. In other words, the good results could have been great results if the right behaviors had been executed. If sales actually grew by 10 percent, they may have grown by 15 percent with good execution. And herein lies the trap. Managers can be seduced by the good results and back off on their management responsibilities, moving on to other situations where they think they are more needed to fix problems. But improving one part of the business from 10 percent growth to 15 percent has the same overall impact as improving another part of the business from negative 10 percent to negative 5 percent (assuming the two parts of the business are the same size, of course). And the impact should be easier to achieve in the part of the business where behaviors are worse.

The bottom right box in the grid represents situations where good behaviors lead to bad results. In this case, the trap is in the definition of bad results. For example, comparing results unfavorably to some higher expectation would be clearly bad. But comparing those same results to what would have happened without the good behavior might put the "bad" label into a different light. Let's look at the selfish driver situation from our own perspective. We do the good thing and stay in our lane while the selfish driver exhibits bad behavior. Our initial feeling is that we have received a bad result; we are later than the other guy. But what alternative behavior might we have pursued? We might have tried to race ahead of the selfish driver to cut him off. That might have satisfied us emotionally for a few minutes, but it might also have resulted in him crashing into our vehicle, or it could have caused a violent road rage incident, or it could have raised our own anxiety level and made us a long-term victim of the rat race. All of those would have been worse results than being a few seconds later than we otherwise would have been. So this bottom right box teaches us to assess the result relative to what would have happened if we had not pursued and executed good behaviors.

Another possibility from the bottom right box is that the good behaviors just have not yet had a complete chance to deliver the good results. Sometimes it takes a while for behaviors to take effect. You don't lose fifteen pounds on the first day you eat a salad for lunch instead of a burger and fries. The impact of consuming less calories will not be visible for some time, but that doesn't mean the good behavior isn't working or isn't taking you in the right direction.

In summary, the Behaviors–Results Grid is another way to express the point that great results come from execution, not just good ideas. When we execute well, good things happen. In addition, this model helps managers focus on the right actions, not just the results. That can be an important benefit in establishing a team culture that everybody can feel good about and will want to be a part of. But let's make this a bit more complicated.

Behaviors, or execution, are not simply good or bad. That would be too easy, and it would make for a very short book. Execution is better viewed as a continuum from 0 percent to 100 percent, with the vast majority of situations falling somewhere between zero and one hundred. To be more accurate, execution is actually two separate continuums set against each other. Consider the following image.

Figure 1.3: The Execution Continuum Chart

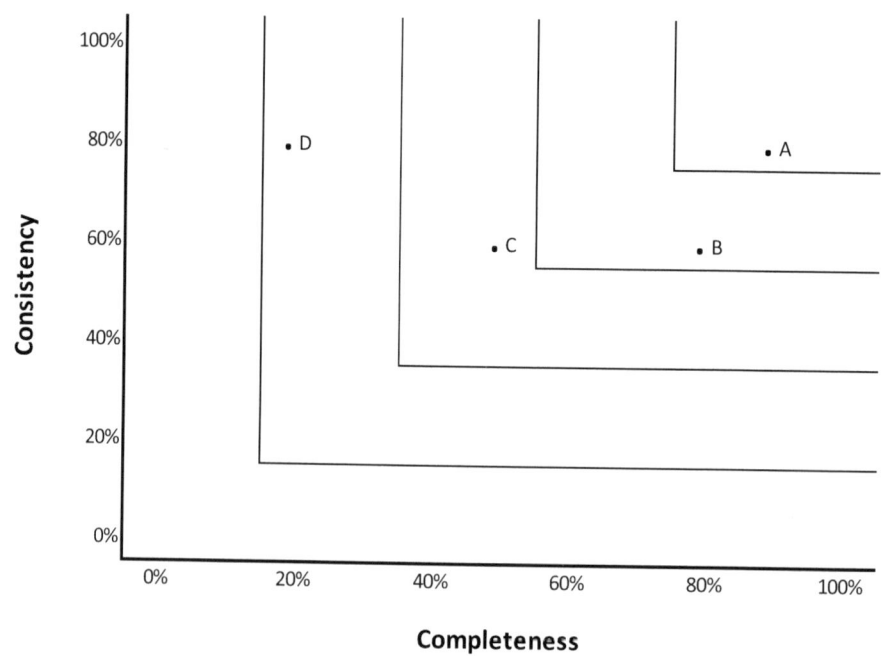

The Execution Continuum Chart plots the two components of execution, completeness and consistency, against each other.

Allow me to explain by breaking down Point D on the chart. This point represents a situation where execution occurs 80 percent of the time, but it is only 20 percent complete. For example, assume the closing staff in a store is required to clean the restroom before they leave for the night. Point D represents a situation where they do remember to clean it 80 percent of the time, but they are only 20 percent complete in doing all that is required for the job of cleaning the restroom (i.e., scrubbing the toilet, cleaning the sink, mopping the floor, refilling the paper towels, refilling the soap dispenser, etc.). This level of execution is in the second tier of the chart.

Let's move on to Point C in the chart. This point represents a situation where the consistency of execution is 60 percent, so less than that of Point D. But the completeness is 50 percent, much better than that of Point D. Point C is in the third tier of the chart, so it is a step better than our first example. Point B moves further to the top right with the same 60 percent consistency but a much better completeness at 80 percent. And Point A is better yet with 80 percent consistency and 90 percent completeness.

This chart is not meant to actually be used in practice. It is simply a way to demonstrate a few important concepts. First, execution is a function of both consistency and completeness. Second, the best execution is that which is highly consistent and highly complete (i.e., the top right part of the grid). And third, assessing the level of execution is far from a simple "good" or "bad;" instead, there is an infinite number of combinations on the consistency–completeness continuum.

This leads to an all-important realization. Achieving 100 percent perfect execution is very hard and rarely done. Sure, getting something done correctly one time isn't that difficult. But getting multiple things done completely, all at the same time, day after day? That's a very different story for so many reasons:

- There are almost always external factors that are out of a team's control.
- Random chance plays a part in many tasks and projects.
- Tasks are not done in a vacuum; there are other priorities competing with the team's time, attention, and focus.

- Unknown obstacles can pop up out of nowhere.
- Staff commitment to the tasks at hand is variable.

So it's often the case that some things get done completely while others are only partly completed. Or some things get done sometimes, and other things get done at other times. It's like the carnival game Whac-A-Mole where participants furiously bang away with a mallet at plastic "moles" that randomly pop up out of five holes. Sometimes you get the mole; sometimes you don't.

I, for one, am glad it's so hard to achieve 100 percent execution. Why? Because I would not have been able to build a successful career in management if it were easy. Think about it. If all it took was to tell people what you want them to do and then sit back and let them do it, there would be little need for good managers. Direction could be issued from a central headquarters office, and everything would automatically happen. In reality, it requires managers to drive execution. Frontline managers, those who supervise the staff on the front lines of the business (i.e., the staff who deal directly with customers) make the difference between inconsistent, incomplete execution by the team and consistently complete execution. Said another way, if execution is the amazing link between good ideas and great results, then frontline management is the type of metal that determines the strength of that link. Effective management is like a link made of steel while ineffective management is like a link made of tin (gold is actually considered a weaker metal, but that would have made for an odd analogy). A steel link means strong execution while a tin link means soft, unreliable execution.

A story from my personal experience further illustrates the important role that frontline management plays in the quality of execution. I was leading a retail business that had its stores located primarily in airports. We had recently expanded the brand into shopping malls all around the US. Some of the mall expansion locations were performing exceptionally well, and others were falling short of sales targets. Before continuing with the next phase of the expansion, we thought it would be a good idea to analyze the stores and find the common thread(s) that made the good locations good. We looked at the shopper demographics of each mall, the anchor stores in each mall, the position of our stores in the malls, the format of our stores (i.e., kiosk vs. in-line), each mall's proximity to an international airport, and several other factors. We could not find a single variable that consistently correlated with either good performance or bad performance. So we decided to take a different approach. We started with the top performing mall location and tried to determine what made it so special. After lots of discussion, we decided that we had to remove the top location from our analysis as an outlier because of the outstanding manager who oversaw the store. We decided the same for the second best and third best locations. Sensing a pattern, we moved to a discussion of the worst performing location. You guessed it—it also was an outlier but this time because the manager had a track record of being a poor supervisor and leader. Voila! The magic variable we were seeking became apparent. The quality of the manager was the one variable that was strongly correlated with our mall stores' success or lack of success.

    I have since come to accept this reality for most businesses. Strong managers find ways to be successful, and weak managers fail to achieve similar levels of success. But why is that? How can one person, the manager, make such a difference with a team that consists of many other people? Why can't a group of good employees do just as well without a good manager?

    The answer is that good managers make it easier for employees to execute. Referring back to the point I made just a few paragraphs ago, there are a whole lot of reasons why consistently complete execution is hard. The purpose of a manager is to guide the team through all of the challenges and obstacles and lead them to good execution. Note that this means that managers don't actually deliver results themselves. Okay, there may be part of a manager's job that involves some degree of individual contribution, but that's not the main function of a manager. The team members are there to interact with customers and deliver the real results. And most team members want to be successful. Very few show up to work every day with the intention of sabotaging the employer that pays them. But success isn't always easy for every member of the team. Managers exist to help team members execute and achieve success.

    Google is an organization that, from its start, took pride in hiring the smartest, most self-motivated talent in the world. Google engineers resented the idea that they needed managers, and Google cofounders Larry Page and Sergey Brin set up a structure in the company's early days that valued empowerment and independence over management structure. The logic was that if they hired the best people and left them alone to collaborate and do their stuff, they would achieve the pinnacle of innovation and creativity. In fact, in 2002, they moved to a flat organizational structure that had no managers. This experiment failed miserably after only a couple of months because too many staff members were running to Page for help with various issues and problems. (Garvin, 2013)

Several years later in 2009, Google kicked off Project Oxygen. The objective of this project was to gather data on the degree to which management mattered in employee performance and to learn the management behaviors that were most closely correlated with superior team performance. After more than ten thousand observations across one hundred variables reported in a four hundred-page analysis, the conclusion was clear. Management does in fact matter; it matters a lot. Google went on to use their data to create a structured and successful management development program that is still in use today. (Bryant, 2011)

Another study published in 2015 came to equally compelling results. Two researchers at Gallup, Jim Harter and Brandon Rigoni, produced a paper titled "State of the American Manager; Analytics and Advice for Leaders" that contained analysis covering 27 million employees across 1.2 million manager-led units over four decades. Two important findings were that managers account for 70 percent of the variance in employee engagement scores, and teams in the top quartile for employee engagement deliver 22 percent higher profitability than teams in the bottom quartile of engagement. This is a very important connection. Employees execute most completely and most consistently when they are highly engaged. If managers account for the majority of employees' engagement level, then managers are directly responsible for the level of employee execution. (Beck & Harter, 2015)

So the point is made. Execution is the link between good ideas and great results, and high-quality management is the thing that makes that link strong. But what exactly do managers do to maximize execution?

Managers perform lots of behaviors and actions. The important actions that are most critical to maximizing team execution can be grouped under four categories of management behaviors. Those categories are:

- Communicate
- Motivate
- Follow up

- Grow talent

These categories are relevant not for the management actions themselves but for the impact the actions have on the members of the team. This is a very important point. Management activities that do not fall into one of these four categories do not directly improve execution. For example, managers are often expected to spend time analyzing their business. Business analysis does not improve execution. Only those activities that have a direct impact on employee activities improve execution. Communicating the results of the business analysis may indeed effect employee behavior and therefore execution. But it's the communication that makes the difference, not the analysis.

In each of Chapters 3, 4, 5, and 6, I will take one of these categories and explore the most relevant management behaviors in detail. I will explain the connection between each management behavior and employee behavior. And, most importantly, I will provide advice on how the management behaviors can be most effectively performed to maximize execution. But first, in Chapter 2, I will discuss the importance that positive professional relationships have for a manager's effectiveness.

Before proceeding into the details of how managers use these behaviors to maximize execution, I need to make one more important point. Consistent execution is not really about delivering business results. In fact, positive business results are a by-product of the managers' quest to improve execution. The most direct beneficiaries of managers' efforts are the team members themselves. Everything that managers do is done with the objective of helping their teams achieve success. The greater success the team has, the better team members feel and the more engaged they become in their roles. That leads to even higher levels of success in the future, creating a virtuous cycle of ever-improving execution. Team members reap the benefit of intrinsic and extrinsic rewards that go along with the pattern of success. Customers also benefit from consistent team execution. As the team successfully executes the company's plans, customers receive the best of the company's products and services. They become more loyal to the company, buy more from the company, and refer the company to family and friends. As a result of all of this positive energy from employees and customers, the company benefits through higher sales and profits. So as you read this book, I encourage you to view the manager's role in driving execution from the perspective of helping team members achieve success and trust that doing good things for team members will result in good things for customers and the company. Everybody wins with consistently good execution, but it starts with a genuine management desire to help employees.

I have one more important introductory point to make about the manager's role. If the manager exists to help team members achieve successful execution, it follows that when team members are unsuccessful, the manager is at least partially at fault. Readers who are reading this book with the hope that they will learn new ways to hold employees accountable for their failure to execute will be disappointed. The real lessons are about managers holding themselves accountable to improved management behaviors that will provide true help to the members of their teams in their quest to execute completely and consistently. This is a theme I will return to several times in the chapters ahead. My mission is to lead readers through a paradigm shift in which they come to accept that poor execution is a byproduct of poor management. Said differently, the quality of a team's execution is directly related to the quality of that team's management. I strongly encourage readers to adopt this mindset in order to get the most value from this book.

Now that we have covered the basic foundation, we're ready to move on to the detail. As you read each section, consider how it works with the sections that have preceded it. I will frequently connect points that complement each other, and I expect you will find there is considerable overlap among the topics we will cover. Let's get dig in.

Chapter 2: The Power of Positive Professional Relationships

Before a leader can hope to effectively perform the four key management behaviors and drive execution with their team, she or he must understand and commit to the power of positive professional relationships. Positive professional relationships provide many benefits on the job. First, managers will achieve more when other people are willing and happy to work with them. Second, managers will get more help and support from others when they need it. Third, managers will earn and retain a more favorable reputation at work. And fourth, managers will experience less stress and pressure on the job. So there are plenty of good reasons for managers to commit to creating positive professional relationships.

I'll make the case for the power of positive professional relationships another way. I ended the last chapter by stating there are four categories of management actions that directly impact team execution: communicate, motivate, follow up, and grow talent. Do you think that a positive relationship makes it more or less likely that…

>…communication with another person will be effective?
>…attempts to motivate another person will be effective?
>…follow-up on the actions of another person will be freely accepted?
>…attempts to develop another person will be effective?

Of course, the correct answer in all four cases is that a positive relationship will make the desirable outcome more likely. And, if those desirable outcomes are more likely and they lead to better execution, it follows that it's in a manager's best interests to strive for positive relationships.

I need to make a distinction between professional relationships and personal relationships. Though the line often becomes blurry when coworkers become "friends," these two types of relationships are not the same. The word "relationship" generally prompts people to think about emotional ties or connections, and that feels very personal. But the word can also have a more businesslike definition as in an association or involvement between two entities. Professional relationships differ from personal relationships in the following three important ways.

1. Whereas the purpose of personal relationships is to maximize one's own satisfaction and enjoyment of life, the purpose of professional relationships is to generate results for the company. The at-work association between individuals does not exist to create personal satisfaction other than whatever satisfaction is consistent with the objectives of the business. For this reason, individuals do not have the option to choose whether to have positive professional relationships or not; they are obligated by their employer to do so.
2. While each individual is free to choose the people with whom they wish to have personal relationships, they have no such choice with professional relationships. People at work are expected to have positive relationships with customers, coworkers, bosses, subordinates, business partners, etc. And that's the case whether they like those people or not.
3. The key components of each type of relationship are different. A key component of a personal relationship may be "love," but that is obviously not a factor in professional relationships. In fact, there are even multiple types of personal relationships, and the key components of those can be very different. For example, a father–son relationship has different key components than a wife–husband relationship. I will talk about the key components of professional relationships in a few minutes.

The relationship gap between managers and employees they supervise is, or should be, even more distinct than the gap between work peers. While the line between personal and professional can be justifiably blurrier between work peers, it's advisable for managers to keep relationships with subordinates more professional than personal. This is because the purpose of the manager-subordinate relationship is to facilitate execution and thereby deliver business results. Personal relationships exist, in part, to ward off loneliness, but leadership, when performed correctly, can be very lonely. Consider the following rules of leadership loneliness:

- Leaders must always take responsibility for their mistakes and for those of their team. Owning up to failures demonstrates integrity and is an acknowledgement of humanness. Taking responsibility for team mistakes earns trust and makes it safe for team members to take accountability for their own actions.
- Leaders must sometimes give feedback that people don't want to hear. It might be feedback about the way they performed on a particular task or general feedback on job performance. It isn't pleasant to give people bad news, especially when those people are not self-aware enough to know for themselves. The responsibility to do so falls on the leader.
- Leaders must sometimes go against the crowd in order to do what is best. In some situations, the entire team might favor a particular course of action, but the "right" action—legally, morally, or per company policy—is different. It is the leader's responsibility to take the right action regardless of what the crowd wants to do and to find a way to help the crowd accept and live by the decision.
- Leaders must always hold themselves to a higher standard of behavior if they wish to retain the respect of those they supervise. With all eyes on the leader, the team takes its cues on how to behave from how the leader behaves. The effective leader ensures that she or he is not used as an example for bad behavior by others.
- Leaders must sometimes make tough choices that leave people sad or angry. Every good team is comprised of people who have differing ideas and opinions. When it's time to make a hard decision between different options, the leader must be decisive even if some on the team do not like the decision.
- Leaders must sometimes tell people "no." No, you can't spend that money. No, you can't have a raise. No, you can't have that promotion. No, you can't hire three extra people. No, you can't run that controversial ad campaign. And these are just a few examples. But with the "no" leaders should provide honest, compelling explanations that help people understand and accept the decision.

- Leaders must sometimes not tell a joke even if it's sure to get a laugh. Some say there is an element of truth in all humor. Whether that is accurate or not, a joke that has a member of the team as the victim takes on a whole different meaning when the boss tells the joke. Team members will look for hidden meaning in every joke a boss tells.
- Leaders must always stay out of the rumor and gossip business. It can be tempting for a manager to share hints of insider news. It admittedly feels good to have people cling to every word. Wise leaders realize that those people are attracted to the news, not to the person sharing it.
- Leaders must not allow themselves to become aligned with one subset of the team. If a leader goes to lunch with the same three people every day, the other ten people on the team will feel they are at a disadvantage. That can lead to charges of favoritism, and because we tend to favor those with whom we spend the most time, the charges might actually be legitimate.

Leadership can be an especially tricky situation for people who are promoted into a managerial role in which they supervise coworkers with whom they were peers. Chances are good that while they were peers with some of these coworkers, they developed personal relationships. Because the emphasis must switch from personal to professional, the dynamics of the relationship must change. It can be hard for the new manager to make the switch, and it can be hard for the ex-peers to understand and accept. But it must happen if the new manager is to be effective at driving consistent execution from the team. One key to making it happen is for there to be honest communication between the manager and the ex-peers. They must openly talk about the new dynamic, and they must freely discuss their concerns. This includes concerns about the potential degradation of personal friendships, concerns about the manager playing favorites among employees, concerns about employee-friends taking advantage of the personal relationship, etc. The personal friendships can continue, but the manager must commit to playing the role of boss and leader while at work, and the employees must commit to acceptance of that new role for their friend.

One truth exists with all relationships, personal and professional. A person only has control over her or his own actions. Nobody has control over another individual's personality, attitude, or intelligence. Sure, one can influence the attitude and actions of others, but they do not have direct control. This is particularly important to remember for managers who are trying to build and maintain positive professional relationships. When another person doesn't respond positively in the context of a personal relationship, one has the freedom to give up and forget about the relationship. No such freedom exists with professional relationships. A manager has an obligation to her or his employer to attempt to build positive relationships at work, whether they like or respect every coworker or not. And it is in a manager's best interests to do so for all of the reasons I listed at the beginning of this chapter. Therefore, every manager is advised to focus on what she or he can control—his or her own actions toward building positive professional relationships—and not be thwarted from that effort by an apparent lack of commitment from others to do the same.

Strategies do exist for times when a manager is faced with a co-worker or an employee who is less willing to do his or her part in building a positive professional relationship. First, the manager should try to determine the root cause of the other person's indifference or resistance. It's difficult to fix a problem when the source of the problem is unknown. The best way to determine the root cause is to have a candid conversation about it. While it may be uncomfortable, greatest success will come from direct, open discussion. The manager should schedule time in advance for the discussion, and the topic must be clear so the other person can be fully prepared and will not feel blind-sided when the conversation starts. The manager must be careful in the setup and in the actual conversation to avoid blaming the other person for the problem. An effective setup might sound something like, "Jon, I sense that we may have gotten off on the wrong foot with each other. It's important to me to have a positive professional relationship with you, so I'd like to talk with you some time in the next couple of days about what I can do improve my part." During the conversation, the manager must listen carefully and remain open to all that the other person has to say. It's possible the other person doesn't even feel there is a problem. In any case, initiating a conversation is an important step, and it is considerably better than remaining quiet and allowing resentment to build up.

I assume by now that you accept (if you didn't before starting this chapter) that positive professional relationships are an important part of ensuring a manager's "metal" is strong enough to create an amazing execution link. Let's transition to a discussion of how a manager creates positive professional relationships. Positive professional relationships possess three critical components, and managers must do their best to embed these components into their relationships at work. I like to call the components the "Three *P*'s." They are as follows:

Positive professional relationships are PLEASANT. This starts with the use of words, tone of voice, and body language that are polite and respectful. Common courtesy words such as "please" and "thank you" are a minimum requirement. Respectful tone and body language include other common courtesies such as good eye contact, appropriate volume, encouraging facial expressions, etc. Pleasant interactions are mostly painless and easy, and they are interactions that people look forward to. It's a good bet that a relationship is not positive if one party feels dread at the thought of interacting with the other party. Individuals with even a minimal amount of emotional intelligence are able to sense if another person does or does not have their best interests in mind. A pleasant relationship is one in which both parties truly care about protecting the interests of the other and that reality is understood by both.

Positive professional relationships are PRODUCTIVE. This means that interactions are beneficial in terms of providing advice, information, or support. Productive interactions result in solutions, or at least progress toward solutions, rather than additional problems. When both parties correctly and consistently feel they will be better off after an interaction with the other party than they were before the interaction, the relationship can be considered productive.

Positive professional relationships are PRINCIPLED. At a minimum, principled relationships are those that involve honest and genuine communication. Both parties feel they can trust the other to tell the truth. The parties share a safe presumption that they will each do what they say they will do and will follow through on commitments they make. And there is mutual trust that privacy will be maintained to whatever extent it is expected or agreed upon.

There is some potential for contradiction among these "Three *P*'s," though the contradictions can be resolved through an application of good judgment. For example, principled communication that is genuine and honest may require delivering bad news or giving critical feedback. Neither of those things are likely to be pleasant, so a conflict appears to exist. But there are many ways to deliver bad news or critical feedback. Within a positive relationship, the delivery is done in a way that is as pleasant as possible given the circumstances, and it fits the model of caring and protecting the interests of the other person.

In summary, positive professional relationships serve as an important starting point for managerial effectiveness. Managers increase their success rate in achieving the amazing link of consistent execution by investing time and energy into building positive relationships with the members of their teams and others at work. But positive relationships alone will not make it happen. Managers must effectively use the four key behaviors to truly drive execution. We're now ready to explore those behaviors in the next few chapters.

Chapter 3: Communicate

"Communicate" is the first, and perhaps most fundamental, of the management behaviors that tie directly to team execution. The reason is simple. Team members cannot execute if they don't know what must be executed. It is the manager's job to pass information about the things to be executed from the company to the employees.

Why can't companies communicate directly to the employees through corporate messages? Well, they can, and most companies do. The problem is that corporate emails and other types of blanket communication aren't effective on their own for several reasons, including the following:

First, employees don't always read corporate emails or watch corporate videos. A manager's first responsibility is to ensure all members of the team are receiving corporate communication.

Second, many employees will have questions after reading or viewing corporate communication. The manager must interpret corporate communication for employees and must fill in the gaps of incomplete corporate messages and reconcile differences between conflicting corporate messages. Without a manager playing this role, employees would all interpret communication in their own ways, and team execution would undoubtedly suffer from the resulting confusion.

Third, managers must help employees sort and prioritize all of the information that comes from corporate messages. In the absence of management prioritization, each team member will make his or her own decisions about which message is most important or most urgent, and again, team execution will suffer from the confusion.

So management communication is foundational to good execution.

There are three key types of things that managers must communicate: general information, goals, and direction. I'll now explore these three categories in detail.

General Information

The category of general information includes all of the background that employees need to know in order to be able to do their jobs. This includes things like the following:

- Work schedule;
- Company policies and procedures;
- Product information, including features and benefits;
- Legal requirements and restrictions;
- Industry news
- Competitor information

Communicating these things is not as simple as just passing each item along to the members of the team as soon as the manager receives them or determines that they must be communicated. In order for the communication to be effective, the manager must be intelligently tactical. Specific tactics that a manager can consider include the following:

Use repeatable communication routines. Some types of non-urgent and/or repetitive information are well suited for routine communication. By "routine," I mean a repeatable pattern that team members can form habits and expectations around. Some examples include the following month's work schedule being posted in the same place on the second Friday of every month, a weekly newsletter that is issued at 9:00 a.m. every Tuesday, or a product update packet that is issued on the first day of each month. Routines such as these help to consolidate information into predictable time slots when employee attention will be greatest and to avoid multiple messages being delivered at random times when employee attention may be weakest.

Use multiple types of messaging. Management communication can occur through paper postings, email messages, group meetings, and one-on-one conversations. There are two good reasons for this. First, different people prefer receiving messages in different ways, and management communication will be effective with the widest audience if it is delivered in ways that best appeal to every member of the team. Some will retain information better if they read it, others if they hear it, and others if it is tailored for them personally. The second reason is that multiple types of messaging means there is a greater chance that the intended audience will receive the message multiple times. That increases the probability of the audience absorbing and retaining the information being communicated.

Filter communication appropriately. Too much of a good thing is a bad thing. That applies to ice cream, sunshine, and communication.

Technology makes the problem worse than it ever has been, and we keep getting flooded with more and more communication every day. Managers are most effective when they can filter out the unimportant messages and narrow the team's focus on the messages that are most important. With less to absorb, less to interpret, and less to think about, team members can devote more thought and attention to the critical stuff that remains.

Get to the point. Just as too many different messages can dilute the focus on the most important messages, too many words in a message can dilute the focus on the most critical part(s) of the message. Make the point, support it succinctly if you have to, and leave it.

Remain open and approachable. Communication isn't only about delivering messages. The most effective communication is two-way, meaning it involves delivering *and* receiving messages. No matter how hard we try, we can't always give everybody all they need in a message the first time. Members of the audience will sometimes have questions or will misinterpret what we say or write. Managers must be open to hear and respond to the questions and must recognize when their communication has somehow missed the mark. By being open and approachable, managers give themselves the chance to learn about and correct misunderstandings.

Goals

The second category of things that managers must communicate is goals. A definition of "goal" is an aim or a desired result. So managers must communicate to employees the results that are desired from their actions. For the purpose of this chapter, I am going to talk about two types of goals: performance standards and objectives. Performance standards are typically the regular, ongoing things that an employee must do on the job while objectives are generally goals that refer to a finite period of time. Let's explore each of these in more detail.

Performance Standards
Performance standards are often written in policy and procedure manuals or in training documents. They may be behavioral in nature, or they can be metric-based.

Examples of behavioral retail performance standards include "employees must acknowledge every customer within three seconds of the customer entering the employee's area of responsibility" and "employees must fix up merchandise displays that have been disrupted by shoppers."

Examples of metric-based performance standards include "employees must sell an average of at least two units per transaction" and "stockroom employees must process at least ten merchandise shipment boxes per hour worked."

These performance standards may change as policies or circumstances change. For example, the standard for minimum units sold per transaction may increase from two to three during the holiday shopping season. In the absence of a communicated change, the performance standards are ongoing.

The purpose of communicating performance standards to employees is so they know how their performance will be measured. I strongly believe that most people want to be successful. In order to achieve success, people need to know what success looks like. Performance standards serve as the goal line that must be reached in order to achieve success. By communicating the standards by which success will be measured, supervisors begin the process of managing to success. For example, if a retail company deems a successful salesperson to be one who averages two units per transaction, and the manager communicates that standard to her sales team, she is one step closer to success than if the team has no idea what the standard is. Having established the standard of two units per transaction, she can now manage the behaviors of the individual salespeople toward that goal.

This brings me to an important caution. The terms "performance standards" and "expectations" are often used interchangeably. There is actually a big difference, and that difference has particularly significant implications on management effectiveness. A standard is something that is used as a measure, a norm, or a model for comparative evaluation. An expectation is a strong belief that something will happen in the future.

Managers can be fond of telling staff they must meet "expectations," but there's never a time when that is a good bar to set. If staff is not already meeting standards on a consistent basis, why would a manager have anything other than an expectation that they will continue to fall short in the future? Telling them to meet expectations is equivalent to telling them to continue falling short of standards. If the team is consistently meeting standards, the manager should be challenging them to perform at a new and higher level. More realistically, the team may be consistently meeting some standards, but it's unlikely they are consistently meeting every standard. In that case, the manager should be thanking the team for the standards they are meeting and challenging them to begin meeting the rest of the standards.

As an example from the world of retail management, a standard might be for a team to give a friendly greeting to every customer. Let's imagine the team typically meets this standard when they aren't working on operational tasks, but they frequently fail to greet customers when they are engaged with other work. The expectation in this case, based on historical precedent, would be that the staff will meet the standard as long as they are not preoccupied with other tasks. In a situation like this, where expectation is short of standard, it is the manager's job to close the gap by managing to the standard, not to the expectation.

The biggest danger of a manager managing to expectations is that the manager begins to accept expectations and stops pushing the staff to meet standards. Whenever a manager manages to expectations and fails to manage to standards, she sends a message to staff that it's okay to fall short of standards. Perhaps the manager begins to believe the standard is impossible to achieve, the manager feels bad about always giving negative feedback, or the manager simply gets tired of pushing the team for more. Whichever is true, the manager needs to take a good look in the mirror and decide whether he or she wishes to be a mediocre manager or a highly effective one. The latter requires a sincere commitment to consistently manage to standards.

One challenge with communicating performance standards is that there are often so many different standards that it's hard for team members to remember them all and to know their relative importance. A typical retail operation has multiple standards for customer service, multiple standards for selling, multiple standards for operational controls, multiple standards for store appearance, multiple standards for business development, etc. How is an employee supposed to know how to prioritize a list of what might be dozens of different standards?

In my first book, *The Retail Management Formula*, I introduced the concept of the Retail Management Pyramid. The Management Pyramid is my solution to this problem of organizing, communicating, and prioritizing all of the performance standards the team must meet. It has proven successful in improving communication and understanding of performance standards, and therefore execution, in businesses that have adopted it all over the world. I'll give only a high-level overview here, and I invite readers who want a deeper dive into the Management Pyramid to read that first book.

The Management Pyramid establishes complete clarity of the key performance standards and clear guidance on the relative importance of all performance standards. It serves as a prioritized list for all team members, and it therefore communicates how team members' behaviors on the job will be measured. The theory behind the pyramid is that the standards at the base (bottom) are those that are most fundamental and critical to the success of the business. These bottom-of-the-pyramid items are typically the most tangible and most objective. That means they are also often the easiest to fix when they are broken. Standards in the middle of the pyramid are a bit more complex. While they are still important, they are more subjective and therefore a bit harder to teach and train. The standards at the top of the pyramid are the "icing on the cake." Said another way, they are the most difficult to implement and the hardest to train. See Figure 3.1 on the next page for an example of a Management Pyramid for a typical retail clothing business.

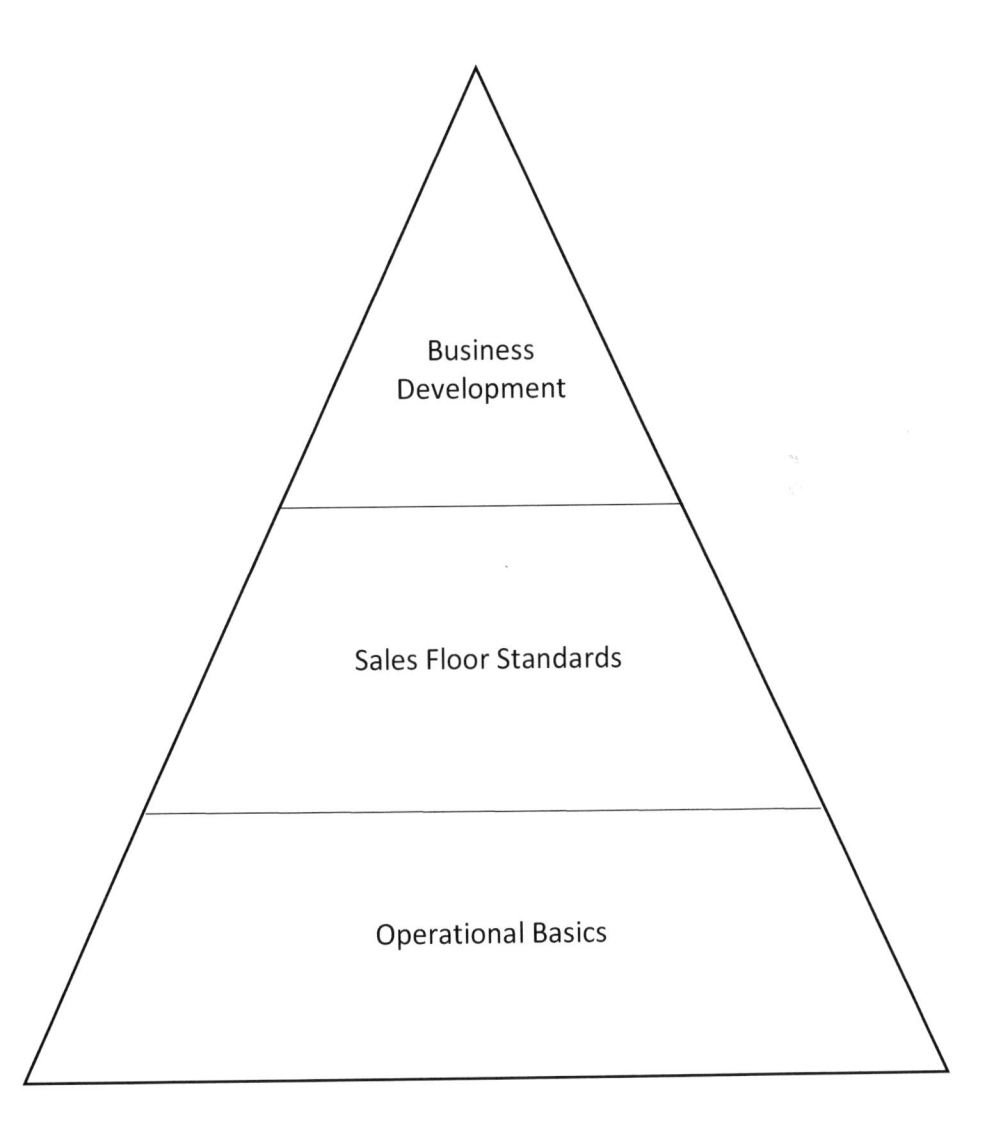

Figure 3.1: The Management Pyramid

Business Development

Sales Floor Standards

Operational Basics

In the example in Figure 3.1, the standards at the base of the pyramid fall into the bucket of "Operational Basics." This includes categories such as

- Cash controls;
- Audit compliance;
- Inventory management; and
- Staffing and scheduling.

The middle tier of standards includes everything related to the sales floor, or the "front of the house." This bucket includes categories such as

- Store appearance;
- Team;
- Customer service; and
- Selling.

The top tier of standards is dedicated to more complex business development standards. This bucket includes categories such as

- Strategic inventory decisions;
- Community relationships; and
- Clientele books.

Once the tiers are established and the broad categories are decided upon within each tier, specific performance standards are added to the pyramid. Standards should be written in the most tangible, specific, and measurable way possible. It's not necessary to explain every detail in the list of standards as this is not meant to take the place of a policy and procedure manual. It's perfectly acceptable for a standard to refer to a particular policy that is detailed elsewhere. Examples of performance standards for the bottom tier of our pyramid might look like this:

Cash Controls
- o Safe is secure and balanced, and only appropriate access is granted.
- o All register tills are balanced and kept in individual control.

- Bank deposits are prepared and taken to the bank daily by 10:00 a.m.
- Cashiers all follow proper procedures for counting money during transactions and counting change back to customers.

Audit Compliance
- Loss prevention policies and procedures are followed.
- Shipment and transfer paperwork is completed accurately and in a timely manner.
- Employee timekeeping is within Department of Labor regulations.
- Operational audit checklist is satisfactory.

Inventory Management
- Shipments are processed per efficiency targets.
- All products are properly represented on the sales floor.
- Fixtures are replenished with all colors, sizes, and appropriate quantities.
- Merchandise is properly tagged and signed.

Staffing and Scheduling
- Proper number and availability of employees are on staff.
- Staff schedule is completed at least four weeks in advance.
- Staff schedule and employee break periods comply with law and with company policy.
- Schedule reflects appropriate staff levels based on anticipated workload.

The same process can be used for the other two tiers of the pyramid. I suggest putting three to five categories into each tier and four to six standards under each category. Fewer than these are an indication that they aren't big enough to stand on their own, and they probably should be combined with other categories or standards. More than these recommended numbers will make it hard to remember and hard to focus.

Prioritization via the tiers is important because it gives team members and managers an order with which to approach and assess the business. In the example above, operational basics form the base of the pyramid, and cash controls have been assigned top priority. That makes sense because good merchandising, good customer service, and good selling skills will all be for naught if the cash generated is given away through poor controls. And inventory management is lower on the pyramid, and therefore more fundamental, than selling skills because even highly skilled sellers can't sell if there is no merchandise on the sales floor to sell.

Team members use the pyramid to know exactly what performance standards they must meet and to guide their decisions on the order in which to focus their efforts. For example, given a choice between spending time to get new merchandise out to the sales floor or spending that time standing on the sales floor to sell, this pyramid guides team members to focus efforts first on getting the merchandise out. Of course there will always be unique details that must factor into these types of decisions. Focus might change if the new merchandise is low-priced add-on items and customers on the floor are ready to buy high-priced top-selling items. In that case, it might be better to focus on helping the customers first before worrying about the new merchandise. So the pyramid isn't meant to take the place of common sense management in the moment. But it does provide general guidance to team members about the order of priorities.

Once you have built the pyramid and its list of prioritized performance standards, it can serve as an effective assessment tool. In fact, it would be a mistake to use anything other than the pyramid to assess the team's behavioral performance. If the pyramid represents the list of important standards you want the team to execute, why would you measure their performance by any method other than comparing it to the list of standards in the pyramid?

One way to use the pyramid as an objective evaluation tool is to turn it into a scoresheet that assigns higher values to the items at the base of the pyramid and lower values to the items at the top. Using our example above, the categories in the Operational Basics tier of the pyramid— cash controls, audit compliance, inventory management, and staffing and scheduling— might be worth ten points each. The categories in the middle tier of Sales Floor Standards—store appearance, team, customer service, and selling— could be worth seven points each. And the categories in the top tier of Business Development—strategic inventory decisions, community relationships, and clientele books—might be worth five points each. That would mean a total of eighty-three possible points. Each category is evaluated, and if performance is satisfactory, the points for that category are awarded while unsatisfactory performance yields zero points for the category. When evaluating a category partial points can be awarded, though I recommend caution with that practice. It's best to send a clear message about whether performance is satisfactory or unsatisfactory, and partial points have the potential to send a message that can easily be misinterpreted. That said, partial points can be used to mark progress from previously unacceptable performance or to mark execution that has been good at times but inconsistent. The team's score is the total number of points awarded divided by eighty-three possible points.

A pyramid evaluation tool such as the one I just described is a standardized way for senior managers to assess performance of multiple teams and multiple managers. But this type of tool is also a great way for managers to do self-evaluations of their operation and of their own effectiveness as the leader of the business. It's very easy for managers to lose objectivity in assessing their own location because they grow to accept rationalizations for why things are the way they are. For example, a manager may have his own justifiable reasons for why the bank deposit can't get to the bank by 10:00 a.m. every day (insufficient staffing, shipment arriving at 9:00 a.m., etc.), so he begins to assess his own performance in handling daily deposits as satisfactory despite the fact that they don't get to the bank until 1:00 p.m. That's a self-deluding assessment because no matter what the rationalization, the standard is not being met. A clear and specific list of measurable standards helps keep managers objective in their self-assessment of the operation.

When using the pyramid as an evaluation tool, it's important to follow the prioritized order of the pyramid. The point of assessing isn't to give a grade or a score. It's to identify things that need to be fixed in order to improve operation of the business. And if there is time to fix only one thing, that time should be spent on the most important thing that needs to be fixed. It would be a mistake to spend time fixing a business development standard from the top of the pyramid when an operational basic from the bottom of the pyramid is also in need of repair. And let's face it—a manager's time is precious, and he can get pulled away from anything on a second's notice. So the amount of time available for the process of assessing can itself be limited. Therefore, in order to ensure the most critical shortfalls in performance vs. standard are identified and fixed, the assessment should proceed from the most important to the least important.

In summary, the Management Pyramid is an incredibly helpful tool for organizing and communicating performance standards, the first type of goal that managers must communicate. Managers use the pyramid to structure their inspection of the business and of the team behaviors, both in terms of what to inspect and in which order. In these ways, the pyramid serves as the primary way for managers to communicate with their team about performance standards.

Performance Objectives

The second type of goal that managers must communicate is performance objectives. While standards refer to regular, ongoing goals for performance, objectives generally refer to finite periods of time. Objectives can be hourly, daily, weekly, monthly, annual, or any other defined time block. They often take the form of sales targets or productivity targets.

Objectives help drive execution because of a concept I mentioned just a few paragraphs ago: most people want to succeed. When there is no definition of what success looks like, team members float through their days without a clear vision of where they are headed. Objectives provide the definition of success they can work toward, and the clear vision of success helps to fuel the team's drive to achieve success.

For an example, consider the story of Florence Chadwick. It was 1952, and Chadwick was attempting to swim the twenty-two miles from Catalina Island to the mainland of California. She had previously become the first woman to swim the English Channel both ways. Now, she was fifteen hours into her Pacific Ocean swim. The weather was foggy, and though there were boats accompanying her, she could barely see them. Several times she expressed to the people on the boats that she couldn't go on, but they coaxed her to continue. Finally, she decided she couldn't swim any more, and she had her handlers pull her out of the water onto one of the boats. Once on the boat, she could better see through the fog and realized the coast was only a half mile away. Later, in the press conference, she said that if she had been able to see the coast and how close she was, she would have been able to keep swimming and make it to shore. (Alcorn, 2010)

For Chadwick, the coast was her objective. Without a clear view of the objective, she couldn't achieve success, but with a clear view, she would have had the confidence and direction she needed. Business objectives for employees have the same effect. They are the mark to strive for, and because most people want to be successful, employees will put in good effort to meet objectives if the objectives are well communicated.

S.M.A.R.T. Goals

Now that we have explored the two types of goals that managers communicate—performance standards and objectives—I want to introduce an important and often-repeated concept concerning goals. The idea of S.M.A.R.T. goals has been around for many years, and there is some disagreement about who should receive credit for the term. The S.M.A.R.T. goal idea originated from the concept of management by objectives which was introduced by Peter Drucker in 1954 in his book *The Practice of Management*, and the phrase is sometimes attributed to him. While he swims around the idea of S.M.A.R.T goals, Drucker never actually uses the term. The earliest mention of the term I have been able to find is from 1981 in an article by George T. Doran titled "There's a S.M.A.R.T. Way to Write Management's Goals and Objectives." (Doran, 1981) Doran uses the acronym S.M.A.R.T. to describe the characteristics of effective goals. He writes that a smart goal is

- Specific: It targets a specific area for improvement.
- Measurable: It quantifies or suggests a measure of progress.
- Assignable: It specifies who will complete the goal.
- Realistic: It states what can be achieved given existing resources.
- Time-related: It specifies when the results can and should be achieved.

Since 1981, many different variations of this acronym have been used. They employ slightly different word combinations, sometimes substituting "agreed upon" or "achievable" for "assignable," "relevant" for "realistic," or "trackable" for "time-related." No matter the variation, the same general foundation applies. S.M.A.R.T. goals are effective because they have tangible characteristics that make them easy to understand. And making goals easy to understand is a function of communication, the critical management behavior we are exploring in this chapter. When goals are not S.M.A.R.T., they are not communicated well, and they are less effective in guiding team actions (i.e., execution) than they otherwise would be.

Direction

The final category of work-related topics that managers must communicate is direction. Direction is more tactical, more precise, and more singular than a goal. Said another way, a goal is something large that must be achieved over time, whether as a repeatable performance standard or as a major objective, while direction is a specific thing that must be done now or at some specified time in the future. To understand the difference, consider an old joke from comedian Steve Martin. Martin had a bit that started, "I'm going to teach you how to become a millionaire and not pay taxes." Then he would say, "Step One—get a million dollars." Martin had communicated a goal, but he missed the specific direction needed to achieve the goal. It's the same in our daily lives as business managers. We can communicate a goal to our teams such as "Grow sales volume by 10 percent over prior year's volume," but we are destined for failure unless we also communicate the specific steps we want the team members to take in order to achieve that goal.

The first step in giving direction to employees is knowing what needs to be done. That may seem obvious, but it's actually not so simple. Managers must have a keen understanding of the performance standards and of the business objectives, and they must have a sharp eye to be able to see when reality is out of alignment with the standards and objectives.

Often, the biggest challenge for managers is staying in managerial mode. Let's face it—frontline managers are just one step removed from having their main function be execution of the performance standards, and many managers are more comfortable doing that kind of individual work. Therefore, they tend to gravitate toward "doing," and when they do, they stop "managing." In other words, when they get involved in completing tasks, they impair their ability to see what needs to be done. When they can't see what needs to be done, they are incapable of giving direction to the rest of the team. The team's productivity suffers even though the manager is personally producing.

I'll now share three best practices that will enhance managers' ability to know what needs to be done and therefore know what direction needs to be given to the team.

Observe. Visualize the image of a high school football coach talking to the team or a police officer directing traffic or a conductor of an orchestra leading the musicians. Each of these roles requires intense focus on what every person under supervision is doing and how they are performing, and each role requires quick reaction to the events occurring in front of them. The best managers keep their eyes on the action and don't allow themselves to get so caught up in their own tasks that they miss what's going on around them. In a retail environment, this requires doing constant walk-throughs or figure eights around the business since conditions can change very quickly. A manager who consistently walks around and carefully observes everything that is happening is in the best position to see what needs to be done.

Use to-do lists. Even those of us with the best memory can't remember everything all of the time. The more there is to do, the harder it is to remember it all. The solution is simple. Write it all down. But write it all in one place on one to-do list. Random notes on small slips of paper, on multiple Post-it notes, or in multiple notes typed in a smartphone won't help much since you then have to remember where you put all of the notes. Keep one running list of everything that must be done. Not only will it keep you organized, but it will also enable you to keep a record of who you assigned to complete each task. Maintain the to-do list in your phone if that's more comfortable for you than using paper, but keep it all in one list. And add new items to your to-do list as soon as you see them or think of them because you might forget to do so later.

Create checklist routines. This is helpful for a series of tasks that must be done on a recurring basis. For example, a retail store might have several things that must be done every day before store opening, such as preparing the bank deposit, stocking supplies at the cash register areas, setting up the cash tills for the registers, and filling in merchandise on the primary fixtures. Those things can all be combined into one pre-opening checklist, and that checklist can be used to create a routine that the team gets into the habit of performing every day. The more habitual the process, the more likely it will be executed consistently. By having it set up in a formal checklist, the clarity of direction is increased.

By observing well, using to-do lists, and creating checklist routines, managers can get good at knowing what needs to be done and what direction they need to give to the team. Now we're ready to talk about how to effectively give that direction. But before I get into the details of how a manager can be most effective in communicating direction to team members, I want to discuss the difference between two words that are often, and incorrectly, used interchangeably. There is a subtle but important distinction between the words "direct" and "delegate." To direct means to tell another person what you want them to do. To delegate means to invest in another person the authority or responsibility to represent you. The first implies little decision-making freedom for the person being directed while the second implies significant freedom for the person being delegated to.

A couple of dangers exist for managers who delegate rather than direct. First, they risk providing the team member with insufficient information about what exactly needs to be done. Second, they risk forgetting that they, the manager, are still ultimately responsible for the results. Sure, delegating to an employee sounds more benevolent and more appealing than giving an employee direction. It may seem like splitting hairs, but they are not the same thing. While there are appropriate times for managers to delegate, they should reserve delegation for use only in situations where an employee is truly a peak performer with the task being delegated. In this chapter, I will focus on the use of "direct" so as to reinforce the message that managers are generally most effective when they provide specific direction and they retain a strong sense of personal responsibility for the direction they give to employees.

With regard to directing employees, a manager will be most successful if she or he is guided by answering five questions within the direction given. Those five questions are as follows:

1. What exactly needs to be done? The more specific the answer to this question, the better. I have a vivid memory of a time more than twenty years ago when I learned this lesson. I was the manager of a sporting goods store, and I had asked an employee to fill the end cap of a shelving unit with three different golf balls. I made a point of being extremely specific. I instructed the employee to put the Titleist balls on the first shelf, the Top Flite balls on the second shelf, and the Pro Staff balls on the third

shelf. When I returned to inspect the work a couple of hours later, I realized the employee had done exactly the opposite. The Titleist balls were on the third shelf, and the Pro Staff balls were on the first. Since I was sure I had been very specific, I could not imagine how he could have gotten it wrong; until I asked him, that is. He assumed the first shelf was the bottom shelf, not the top one. I had to admit it was my fault. If I had been more specific and used "top shelf" and "bottom shelf" instead of "first" and "third," we would not have had the misunderstanding.

2. Why does it need to be done? People usually want to feel like the work they do has some purpose. The more important the purpose, the greater the feeling of accomplishment when the work is complete. Giving employees the reason for the task helps them to feel good, and that hopefully gets them more invested in completing the task well. But there's an even better reason for telling employees the underlying objective. When employees understand the purpose, there is a better chance they will make appropriate choices as they encounter obstacles or decision points during their completion of the task. And they may even think of a better way to fulfill the objective than the direction the manager has given them.

3. Who needs to do it? It may seem obvious that the person who needs to complete the task is the person to whom the manager is giving direction. But it may not be so obvious to the employee. For example, the employee may take it upon herself to include coworkers in the assignment, as in, "Hey, guys, the manager wants us to do this." The manager must be clear if the employee should complete the task personally and alone, enlist the help of others, or make the decision on whether to do it alone or with help.

4. When does it need to be done? Is the task so urgent that the employee must drop whatever he is working on and complete it now, or is it something that can wait until later? Is the task something that should not be started at all until the current work is finished? Leave these questions unanswered, and a manager is leaving the decision up to the employee. The employee's

decision may not match the manager's desire. And the answer to this time-related question isn't only about when the work should start. It's also about the amount of time it should take and the deadline for having the task completed.

5. How shall it be done? There may be a certain sequence of steps that are necessary to complete the task. Or there may be a faster, more productive way to complete the task. Ironically, one thing I remember most vividly about learning how to operate the cash register at a clothing store had nothing to do with the cash register. I was taught how to quickly remove hangers from shirts by pulling them through the bottom instead of unbuttoning the collar and removing them the normal way. Removing hangers this way wasn't directly related to operating the cash register, but it was an important way to ensure a speedy process that improved customers' experience with the checkout process. Sometimes the process is critical to proper completion of the task, and other times a defined process can improve productivity. Either way, the manager must include process details when giving direction.

When giving direction to an employee, a manager should explain any freedom the employee has to make decisions during her completion of the task. For example, a manager may direct an employee to fill in a fixture with four colors of a shirt, and he may direct that the four colors be white, black, blue, and red. But he may tell the employee, "You can decide the order in which you arrange the colors of the shirts." If the manager has certain criteria he wishes the employee to use in making the decision, he should communicate that criteria. For example, "Please consider customers' preference for each color and put the best-selling colors on the top and the lesser selling colors on the bottom."

After giving direction to an employee and proactively answering the five questions above, a manager should give the employee a chance to ask questions. Even when a manager thinks she has been overly clear and specific, there is a chance the employee didn't understand some aspect of the direction given. It's far better to learn that fact before the task is begun than after the task has been completed incorrectly. It's a good practice for managers to ask employees to recite back the direction they have been given. This will reveal whether employees truly understand the tasks they are given, and it will provide an opportunity to correct misunderstandings right up front. That's a lesson I wish I had learned before my misunderstanding with the golf ball merchandising.

Manager Training Checklist #1—Communicating

These are behaviors or skills that managers should acquire in order to maximize team execution.

- ☐ Build repeatable communication routines that establish expected patterns for team members.
- ☐ Use multiple types of messaging to communicate important messages to the team.
- ☐ Filter communication appropriately and refrain from over-communicating so as to keep messages focused.
- ☐ Remain open and approachable and encourage two-way communication with team members.
- ☐ Manage to "standards," not to "expectations."
- ☐ Effectively use the Management Pyramid as a communication, prioritization, and evaluation tool for performance standards.
- ☐ Communicate performance objectives in the form of S.M.A.R.T goals.
- ☐ When giving direction to team members, use the five-question method (what, why, who, when, how).

Chapter 4: Motivate

"Motivate" is the second key management behavior that links directly to consistent execution. The word motivate means "to provide a cause or a reason to act." That definition can cover a wide range of specific actions including encouragement, incentives, and threats. For example, the threat of physical harm can be an effective motivation for a person to act. In the world of management, threatening physical harm is frowned upon by companies' attorneys and human resources departments. Instead, we tend to focus our definition of motivate on the more positive ways of providing a reason for team members to act.

Before I get into exploring the many different ways that managers can positively motivate team members to execute, I want to address an unhelpful perspective that some managers have. I have heard managers say things like, "Why do I need to motivate employees to do their jobs? Their motivation should be their paycheck at the end of the week!" To take it a step further, why should it be necessary to motivate employees to do the things they know they are supposed to do? Can't it be seen as a bad attitude if an employee needs something extra in order to do what she or he is supposed to do on the job? Indeed, these are reasonable questions, though they do demonstrate a naïve understanding of human psychology.

Perhaps it may be a bad attitude. But any assessment of attitude is relative to different baselines (i.e., attitude relative to other team members, relative to management attitudes, etc.), and whether it is or is not deemed bad attitude, one's assessment doesn't change reality. In other words, one can label it bad attitude, but it's just the way it is. People sometimes need external motivation to do things at work that their managers think they "should" do on their own initiative.

Why is this the case? First, we all draw lines on our priorities in different places. For example, it may be very important to you to excel at your job (you are reading this book, after all!). Another person may put higher importance on building personal relationships, and that may cause him or her to focus more on making friends at work than on executing the boss's direction. Is that person wrong for prioritizing personal relationships over work? There is no right or wrong; it's just two different perspectives on life. In fact, for every person in the US workforce who is designated as being in a management occupation, there are 9.5 who are not. So our perspective as managers, as much as we may think it is right, is a clear minority of the US population. (U.S. Census Bureau, 2004-2005)

A second explanation for why team members might need extra external motivation is that a task or behavior may be particularly more difficult for them than it is for the manager. It's likely the difficulty makes the task or behavior less fun for the team member. For example, an ordinary, healthy person finds it easy to walk a short distance, say from the parking lot to a store entrance. Such a person does not need the extra support of cheering friends and family in order to successfully make that walk. The same ordinary person finds it considerably more difficult to run a half-marathon. External support and cheering from loved ones may be very helpful in keeping that person committed to the challenge. The same holds true, albeit in a less extreme and dramatic way, to tasks at work. A particular task may seem to an experienced manager like a walk from the parking lot to the store entrance, but to a less experienced, less skilled team member, the same task may seem like a half-marathon run. The example may be extreme, but the point is that task difficulty can impact a person's motivation to take on the task, and the perception of task difficulty may be very different between managers and team members.

Though there are many other explanations, I won't drag the point out any further. I will simply recommend that we refrain from judging others about the external motivation they need and instead accept the reality that our team members may not be quite as internally driven to execute company initiatives as we are. Once we accept that reality, we are ready to talk about the many ways that managers can motivate team members. Here are some good practices that can help managers to motivate their team members.

Treat Team Members with Respect
This one is easy to understand. People prefer to be around others who treat them with respect. It follows that people will do more for others who treat them with respect. It's true in personal relationships, and it's true in professional relationships (we covered this in Chapter 2). Managers give themselves a better chance of achieving consistent team execution when they create an environment of respect.

One simple way to demonstrate respect is to use common courtesy words when assigning and following up on task assignments. It may seem silly to have to advise managers to say "please" when asking a team member to complete a task, yet I far too frequently see managers give direction in the form of an order rather than a request. Unless you are employed by a branch of the military, I strongly recommend that you treat assignments to team members as things they have an option to do or not do. Actually, they do have that option. Sure, a potential consequence of them choosing not to do an assigned task is that they may lose their job. But that does neither of you any good. They have no job, and you have nobody to complete that task and the many more that will be necessary during the time you are busy hiring a replacement. So make it easier on yourself; use "please" and "thank you" whenever you assign and follow up on tasks.

I have one important caution when it comes to using common courtesy words. I strongly recommend you avoid the phrase "Please do me a favor." A favor implies that it's personal rather than business, and it implies that you will owe the person a return favor at some point in the future. I know it may seem like a fine line, but there is a difference between asking a team member to complete a task and asking someone for a favor. You are the boss, and that person works for you. Team members have an implicit expectation that you will assign tasks to them; you don't need to ask for a favor. I'm only suggesting in this section that they will be more eager to comply with a request than with an order.

Another way you, as a manager, can treat team members with respect is to refrain from language that reminds them that you are in charge. You may have noticed that I try to use the term "team members" instead of "employees." That is intentional, and it is for this reason. I recommend that managers take the perspective that everybody is on the same team and all are working together. Sure, different members of the team have different roles, and the manager's role is to provide direction to the other members of the team, but that's a less authoritarian perspective than one that highlights the manager as boss and the rest of the team as subordinate employees. Of course, there is sometimes a need for a manager to exert his authority, but the default paradigm should not be "because I'm the boss."

One final suggestion for treating team members with respect is to include them in decision-making to whatever extent it is appropriate. Let's face it—we all will work harder to execute our own ideas than to execute somebody else's ideas. It's obviously not possible for team members to make all of the decisions. In fact, the vast majority of decisions will be made at company headquarters or by local management. Finding a way to give team members some decision-making authority on each task is a true managerial art. Perhaps team members can choose the order in which they complete a set of assignments, or they can choose which team member completes which assignment, or they can decide on some small details of an assignment. The smallest amount of choice can make a big difference in the amount of a team member's buy-in to a task.

One caution: managers must be sure to not give decision-making authority to a team member before she or he has demonstrated the good judgment to make solid decisions of this type. Doing so can cause more frustration than motivation for both you and the team member.

Participate in the Task
A spin-off of the suggestion to treat team members with respect when assigning tasks is to personally participate in the task. This means exactly what it sounds like. Roll up your sleeves and do the task, or part of it, yourself. I have heard many managers state that they never ask a team member to do a task they aren't willing to do themselves. This is admirable, and it shows that you, as the manager, don't feel like you are above doing the things that you are assigning to others. That's especially effective with the unpleasant tasks like cleaning the bathroom or dealing with a particularly difficult customer. Also, it gives you the chance to demonstrate your expertise (assuming you have some), and that will hopefully provide a model for team members to follow in the future.

While there is absolutely a time and place for rolling up the sleeves, I must communicate an important caution regarding this tactic. Everybody on the team has a role, and the manager's primary role is not to perform tasks that are really team members' responsibilities. It is far too common for me to see managers "rolling up their sleeves" while their employees are standing around talking or daydreaming. Participating in the task should be an occasional tactic used for motivational or teaching purposes; it should not be a regular routine. Otherwise, the manager has voluntarily demoted himself, and the company is overpaying for an extra team member who is not needed.

Give Praise and Appreciation

Imagine being a professional baseball player who hit a homerun and thousands of fans cheered. Or imagine being an actress in a Broadway musical who just belted out a powerful solo, and the entire theater clapped. Or remember a time when you were a child in school, and you brought home a particularly good report card and your parents gave positive feedback. In each of these situations, the reaction from others elevated your mood, made you feel like the effort you exerted was worth it, and made you motivated to do it all again.

We humans are in a continuous search for approval from others. The more we respect another person, the more we crave approval from that person. It starts when we are very small children, and it continues throughout our lives. At work, our bosses are in positions of authority over us. Even the most rebellious among us have some level of respect for authority, which means we crave some level of approval from our bosses. Proof is in the fact that receiving praise from our boss makes us feel good and being ignored by our boss after we have done good work makes us feel bad.

The lesson for those of us who are often in the "boss" position is that our actions, or inactions, can make our team members feel good or feel bad. Give praise and appreciation when it is deserved, and we make team members feel good. Fail to give praise and appreciation when it is deserved, and we make team members feel bad. Either way can quickly become a powerful cycle. Give praise; the team member feels good. Good feeling leads to higher motivation that drives more good performance and earns more praise. Or the cycle can spin the opposite way. There are few other things a manager can do that motivates effectively with such minimal investment.

I have one big tip for giving praise. Make sure the praise is specific. Note the difference in the following two examples of praise that a manager might give:

- "You did a great job with that customer! Well done!"
- "You did a great job listening and understanding that customer's true needs! Because you listened so carefully, you were able to match them with a more suitable product than the one they first asked about. Well done!"

The first example is okay, but it's not obvious that the manager was truly paying attention to the team member's interaction with the customer. Yes, there's a general sense that the interaction went well, but the praise isn't fully credible because the team member can't be sure exactly what part of their behavior is being praised. The second example is more effective because it's clear that the manager was paying close attention to the team member's behavior and was able to point to exactly which actions were worthy of praise. The more credible praise is, the more motivating it is for the team member.

Use Monetary and Other Extrinsic Rewards
This is a tricky one. On the one hand, monetary incentives, bonuses, trophies, plaques, and prizes are common methods of motivation in our society. In fact, they are so common that team members often expect those types of rewards as a minimum foundation of their motivation. On the other hand, money and prizes can be so powerful that they drive behaviors that are counterproductive. Consider the following example from my past personal experience.

I was new to the leadership role of an airport-based retail business. I had been told about the company's recently deployed incentive plan that paid meaningful bonuses to frontline sales associates who exceeded their goals for average transaction value. And I had been shown the results of that incentive plan. Average transaction values had indeed grown materially since the implementation of the incentive program. It was hard to argue with the program's apparent success, though nobody could explain to me why overall revenue was not growing along with the increase in average transaction values.

While I was visiting our locations at a major airport, I overheard a sales associate tell a customer that she could not complete the customer's requested transaction because our minimum transaction was fifty dollars. I asked the manager what was going on as I had not yet heard that minimum transaction rule. The manager explained that the sales associate was wrong, and he would take care of it.

I moved on to a different location in the same airport, and I heard the same thing happen with another sales associate and customer combination. That's when I realized that the incentive plan was driving frontline behavior that was costing the company money. Sales associates were turning away small transactions in order to increase their overall average transaction value. And we were paying them bonuses for doing so!

So I endorse the use of incentive plans and contests to motivate team members. But I urge extreme caution to select conditions that will not lead to unproductive behaviors. This includes setting payouts or rewards in a way that will not supersede the company's larger goals. For example, the situation I described above could have been avoided by setting a condition that sales associates had to first meet their overall revenue target before any incentive for high average transaction value would be paid.

One aspect of using extrinsic rewards as a motivational tool that can be very effective is creating healthy competition among team members. Contests can generate fun and exciting rivalry, and that can motivate team members to push themselves to do their best. This is most effective when the contest is of relatively short duration (a couple of weeks or a month at a time), and when different types of contests and different contest themes are used at different times. For example, contest themes can be tied to seasonal events or to specific seasonal business targets. Managers should take care to ensure team members have approximately equal chances of winning, and to vary the measurement methods from contest to contest to ensure fresh motivational power from each.

Another way to promote healthy competition among team members is to maintain tracking charts that rank individuals' results. Most people are motivated by seeing themselves publicly recognized for top performance, and those at the bottom may be spurred to improve their performance so they can rise to the top. Managers must be aware that public posting of individual results may have a demotivating impact on those at the bottom. An ideal way to address this is to post a few different types of results so that every member of the team has a fair chance of being at or near the top of some category.

Set Challenging Targets
Note that I led this section off by saying "set challenging targets," not "set impossible targets." In order for targets to be motivational, they must be neither too easy nor too hard. Too easy, and they fail to push team members to achieve anything more than ordinary results. Too hard, and they create a feeling of defeat before team members even attempt to execute. So when setting targets, use the Goldilocks approach and aim for "just right."

A concept that has gained popularity in recent years is gamification of work. According to TalentLMS, an online learning platform that has more than seventy thousand learning portals, gamification means turning work activity into more of a game-like experience. This includes ideas like earning badges for lessons learned or tasks accomplished, earning points that can be traded for prizes, posting leaderboards, and achieving levels through work successes. Some of the statistics on gamification at work are very compelling. According to a 2019 survey by TalentLMS (Apostolopoulos, 2019),

- 89 percent of employees say gamification makes them feel more productive;
- 83 percent of employees who receive gamified training feel motivated (versus 28 percent who feel motivated when they receive non-gamified training); and
- 87 percent of employees say that game elements make them feel more socially connected and provide a sense of belonging at work.

Gamification can be an effective way to create targets that are not only challenging but also fun to achieve. And gamification can create the healthy competition that we talked about in the last section on extrinsic rewards. Importantly, gamification has the added benefit of not creating a separate source of financial compensation. That avoids the extra cost associated with incentive plans, and it avoids the potential danger of becoming so important that it drives inappropriate or counterproductive team behaviors.

Appeal to a Bigger Team Purpose
One of the most motivating feelings people crave is to know that the work they are doing matters. And the more important the work is, the better the feeling. A 2016 survey of twenty-six thousand LinkedIn members found that 74 percent of candidates want a job where they feel like their work matters. Despite popular beliefs, it wasn't just millennials who felt this way. Baby boomers and Generation X-ers were equally as likely (even more likely) to want a sense of purpose from their work. (Vesty, 2016) As managers, we can get our teams to be more engaged and more committed

to their work if we can find a way to give them the feeling that their work matters.

It may seem like it will be hard to link ordinary team objectives to a truly meaningful purpose, but a team's purpose doesn't have to be saving whales or protecting the rain forests. The purpose can be much closer to home. It can be as simple as restating team objectives from the perspective of how they help people. For example, a salesperson at a teen fashion retail store isn't just selling cheap clothing. She is helping young women and men find fashion that helps them achieve the perfect balance between expressing their individuality and fitting in with the group. A bank teller isn't just cashing checks; he is helping people manage their lives by providing access to money when they need it. A worker at a self-storage facility isn't just renting storage units. She is helping people get through life's stressful transitions as easily as possible. The best thing about these examples is that they are all entirely genuine; they are just presented from a different point of view.

Take an Interest in Team Members Personally
By taking an interest in team members personally, I literally mean to care about them not just as employees but also as people. People feel more comfortable when they are treated like people rather than objects. Think about the people at work, bosses or otherwise, who you have been most willing to do good things for. I'll bet those are the same people who truly cared about you as a person. You are more motivated to go out of your way for others who care about you. It's human nature.

But it's not so easy for managers to take a personal interest in every team member. Managers bear a lot of pressure to produce results and to get things done. That often doesn't leave a lot of time for friendly chit-chat, and even if there was time, managers should draw a line between personal and professional relationships. In addition, all members of the team may not fit the profile that a manager typically looks for in his or her friends. But the most motivating managers somehow find time to know a bit about each person on the team and what makes him or her tick personally. That might include knowledge about that person's family, hobbies, personal background, weekend plans, etc.

I'm not suggesting that managers should pry awkwardly into the personal lives of the employees who work for them. More to the point, I'm not suggesting that managers should make an awkward effort to attain this type of information from team members. There cannot be a checklist for taking personal interest in others.

For example, consider a manager who on Friday makes a point to ask a team member what plans he has for the weekend. The manager checks the box that he took personal interest, and he half listens to the answer. On Monday morning, he asks the same team member what he did over the weekend. He checks another box, thinking he did a good thing. The team member, on the other hand, sees through the entire charade and resents the manager for pretending to care. More harm is done than if the manager never asked at all.

Taking a personal interest must be genuine. If the manager genuinely cared, he would ask the question with the intention of listening and absorbing the information, not checking off a box on a list. If a manager truly cares about those he or she works with, the interest will be demonstrated through regular, unplanned interactions, and team members will innately understand and appreciate the caring.

Another way for managers to take a personal interest in team members is to help them grow in their jobs and careers. This involves honest and direct feedback, and it involves extra time to train and coach. Just as importantly, it involves asking and understanding where they want to go in their careers. We will cover this in more detail in Chapter 6 when we talk about the management behavior "Grow Talent."

The Leadership Balance Model

Think back to experiences you have had with "easy" bosses and "tough" bosses. Or you can think about "easy" teachers and "tough" teachers. Under which bosses or teachers did you do your best work? Your initial reaction to this question is probably that it's difficult to answer. You may have done good work for both types, and you may have also done lesser work under both types. The easy bosses or teachers were more fun, and you undoubtedly experienced less stress. So you may have been happy, engaged, and energetic in the environment that the easy ones created. The tough bosses or teachers asked more of you, and they pushed you to achieve greater things. You probably didn't enjoy the experience as much, but you may have worked harder because you felt like you had to in order to survive.

The reason it's difficult to answer the question is because it's not a one-dimensional issue. In other words, your feelings about a boss or teacher are not one single continuum from easy to tough. It's actually a two-dimensional issue, with the two dimensions being the level of challenge you feel and the level of confidence you feel. While the two may seem to be opposites and we often conflate them in our minds, they are actually separate feelings. You can feel confident and challenged at the same time. And that's when you produce your best results! Take a look at my Leadership Balance Model in the figure below.

Figure 4.1: The Leadership Balance Model.

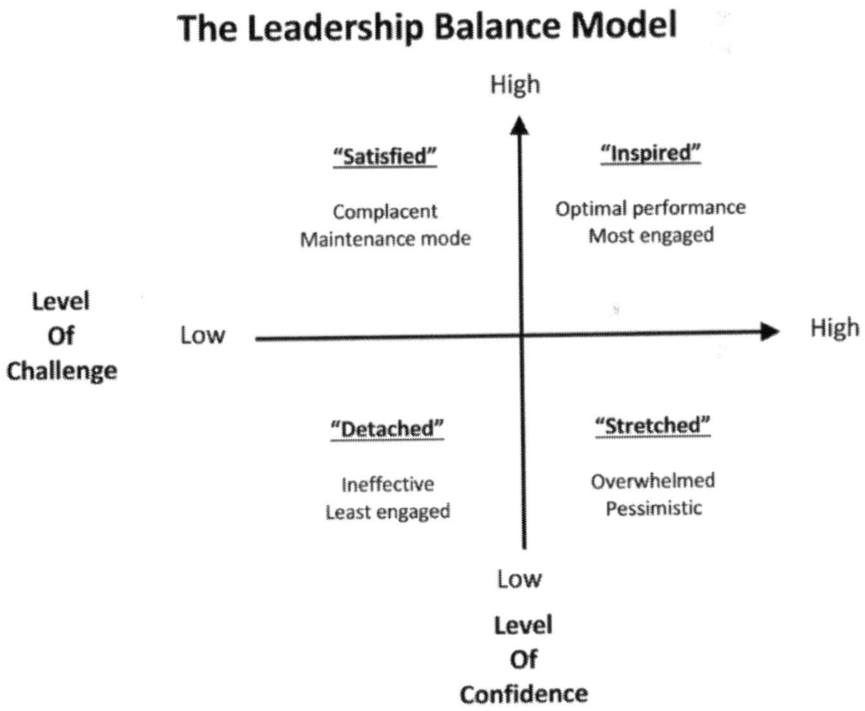

The Leadership Balance Model

Upper-left quadrant — "Satisfied"
Complacent
Maintenance mode

Upper-right quadrant — "Inspired"
Optimal performance
Most engaged

Lower-left quadrant — "Detached"
Ineffective
Least engaged

Lower-right quadrant — "Stretched"
Overwhelmed
Pessimistic

Vertical axis: Level Of Challenge (Low to High)
Horizontal axis: Level Of Confidence (Low to High)

The Leadership Balance Model features four quadrants, each quadrant representing a different blend of challenge and confidence that an employee might feel. There are a couple of key concepts that underlie this model. First, the model assumes that the employee's feeling is at least partially a result of the leadership style used by the manager. Second, the model assumes that employee's feeling is situation specific and can change at any time. Optimal performance and maximum employee engagement are achieved when leaders instill high confidence and high challenge at the same time. Other combinations of confidence level and degree of challenge deliver suboptimal performance and lower levels of employee engagement. Let's explore the four quadrants in detail.

The top left quadrant represents situations where an employee feels high confidence combined with low challenge. This leads to a feeling of satisfaction, and it is created by what I call the "Nice Manager." The Nice Manager makes a point of celebrating every success but fails to challenge team members to higher levels of performance. This is a comfortable place for an employee to be, but that comfort breeds complacency and lack of drive. An employee in this quadrant seeks to maintain the status quo and has little motivation to make changes or to work harder. She or he is satisfied and is likely to coast as long as no material challenge is introduced.

The bottom right quadrant represents situations where an employee feels high challenge combined with low confidence. This is created by what I call the "Merciless Manager," and it leaves the employee with a sense of being stretched. The Merciless Manager always pushes for more and seldom takes time to show appreciation for accomplishments or to acknowledge successes. The pressure to meet challenges may drive some extra short-term effort, but the effort comes from fear rather than positive motivation. Employees in this quadrant feel overwhelmed, and they are apt to be pessimistic about their chances for achieving success on the job. That pessimism eventually leads to lower effort since they think the effort is unlikely to yield positive results in the long run.

The bottom left quadrant represents situations where an employee feels low levels of both confidence and challenge. This is created by what I call the "Hands-off Manager." This management style provides infrequent attention and feedback, leaving employees on their own to manage themselves. Being in this quadrant causes employees to feel ignored, and they eventually become detached if left in this quadrant too long. These team members are the least engaged of all, and that results in the lowest productivity levels. Hands-off Managers who provide employees with insufficient attention, thereby leaving them with low confidence and low challenge, are highly ineffective in getting their teams to execute.

The top right quadrant represents situations where an employee feels high levels of both confidence and challenge. This is created by what I call the "Effective Manager," and it is the best situation for driving long term engagement and results. Employees in this quadrant feel confident in their ability to do their jobs, and they also feel challenged to push for more. The high degree of confidence gives them courage to push themselves beyond their comfort zone. Managers create this situation by continually providing balanced feedback; they praise successes and point out opportunities for improvement.

Inevitably, employees move around these quadrants, depending on their most recent circumstances. A round of positive feedback from the boss moves them higher on the "confidence" scale while the assignment of new and difficult projects moves them higher on the "challenge" scale. While subtle movements along these scales are normal, unpredictable and wild fluctuations between the levels of challenge and confidence will lead to confusion and frustration. For this reason, leaders should aim to make employees feel highly confident in some ways and highly challenged in other ways, and they should strive to continuously maintain that balance over time.

The Tude-O-Meter

One of the hardest things for a manager to address with an employee is attitude. Attitude is a very personal subject, and employees are not likely to be honest with their manager when they have a bad attitude. I designed the Tude-O-Meter to help managers communicate with their team members about their attitudes. Take a look at Figure 4.2 on the next page.

Figure 4.2: The Tude-O-Meter

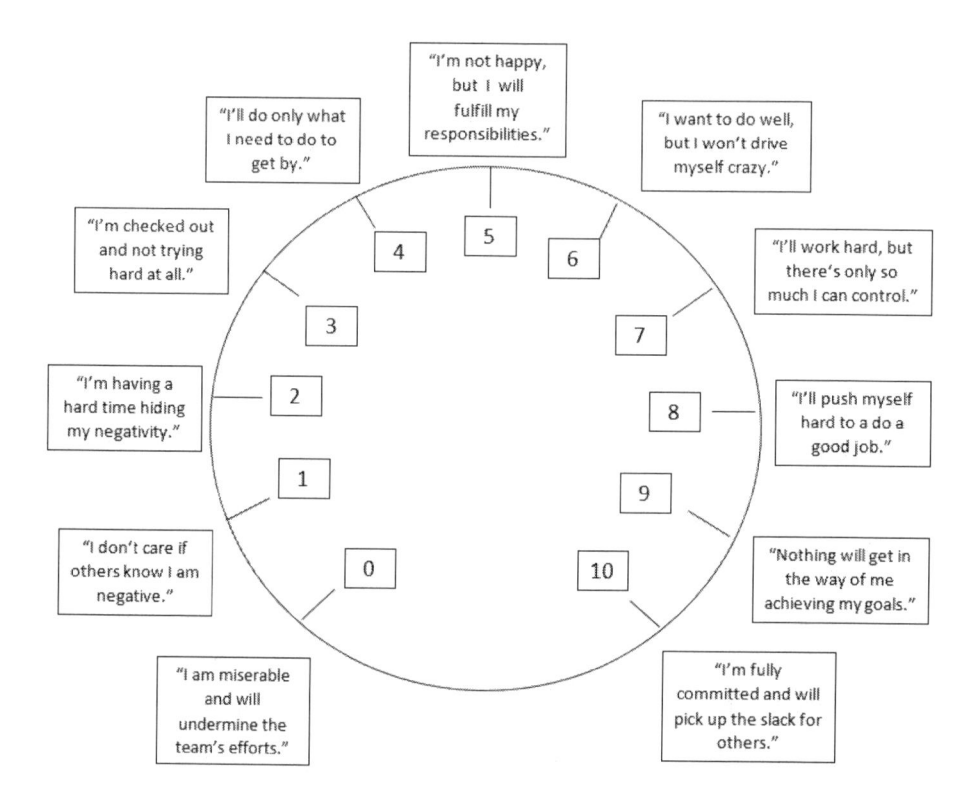

Tude-O-Meter (scale 0–10):

- 0 — "I am miserable and will undermine the team's efforts."
- 1 — "I don't care if others know I am negative."
- 2 — "I'm having a hard time hiding my negativity."
- 3 — "I'm checked out and not trying hard at all."
- 4 — "I'll do only what I need to do to get by."
- 5 — "I'm not happy, but I will fulfill my responsibilities."
- 6 — "I want to do well, but I won't drive myself crazy."
- 7 — "I'll work hard, but there's only so much I can control."
- 8 — "I'll push myself hard to a do a good job."
- 9 — "Nothing will get in the way of me achieving my goals."
- 10 — "I'm fully committed and will pick up the slack for others."

The Tude-O-Meter works by objectifying attitude. In other words, it turns the highly personal subject into an objective conversation. Typically, when a manager tries to address an employee's negative attitude, the employee immediately becomes defensive. He will not acknowledge his bad attitude, or he will deflect and blame others for his bad attitude. It might go something like this:

> Manager: "I feel like your attitude is not positive, and it's causing you to not put in your full effort on the tasks you have been assigned."
>
> Employee: "I do not have a bad attitude. It's just been very busy, and I can't possibly get to everything you want me to do."

64

Manager: "I have seen you in the past work much faster than you have been working lately. It seems like you are not trying as hard as you used to."

Employee: "Well, maybe that's because you expect me to pick up the slack for the others who don't work as hard, and you don't appreciate it when I do."

Of course, this type of conversation might have gone a bit better if the manager started it off in a less combative way. Perhaps a question such as "Are you feeling okay this week? It seems like you aren't working up to your usual level of effort, and I am worried about you" might lead to a less defensive response. But it still places fault on the employee, and the employee will feel a need to defend his or her lack of full effort.

The Tude-O-Meter can take some of the edge off the conversation by pointing the conversation to another object rather than straight onto the employee. Imagine the conversation going like this instead:

Manager: "Where are you at on the Tude-O-Meter today?"
Employee: "I guess I'm about a six."
Manager: "What can I do to help you get up to an eight or better?"
Employee: "It would feel better if I knew you appreciated how hard I always work."
Manager: "That's fair. I'll tell you what. If you can kick it up to an eight this week, Friday's lunch is on me. Deal?"

Sure, it's gimmicky, and it's not for every manager. But it is a way to quantify the motivation level of team members, and it creates a foundation for talking about motivation level with them. It acknowledges the reality that attitude is not constant, and it makes it acceptable for team members to admit when their attitude is less than perfect. Being able to talk honestly and objectively about attitude is the first step toward being able to improve attitude.

For managers who don't like the idea of the Tude-O-Meter, I still suggest honest, direct conversations with team members about attitude. The key is to withhold blame. Discussions about attitude are difficult because they contain an assumption of blame that is placed on the employee. If the conversation can be initiated with a genuine openness to the idea that a team member's bad attitude may be justified, or at least understandable given certain circumstances, then the team member can feel comfortable to speak freely without worry about being negatively judged. That leaves the door open for resolution of whatever problem is causing the bad attitude.

Manager Training Checklist #2—Motivating

These are behaviors or skills that managers should acquire in order to maximize team execution.

- ☐ Consistently treats team members with respect.
- ☐ Gives appropriate praise and appreciation when it is earned, and make the praise very specific with regard to what exactly the team member did so well.
- ☐ Uses good judgment in deciding when to participate in tasks for motivational purposes without voluntarily stepping down from managerial role.
- ☐ Makes effective use of extrinsic rewards to motivate desired behaviors without driving unwanted or harmful behaviors.
- ☐ Sets challenging targets that stretch the team while still being attainable.
- ☐ Effectively keeps team members in the top right quadrant of the Leadership Balance Model; recognizes and reacts whenever they slip into one of the other quadrants.

Chapter 5: Follow Up

If communicating is the management behavior most directly linked to setting up the right conditions for consistent execution, follow up is the behavior most directly tied to ensuring consistent execution actually happens. In fact, as defined by Dictionary.com, the noun version of follow up is an action that serves to increase the effectiveness of a previous action. In the context of management, to follow up means to check in on, or inspect, the result of an instruction that was previously given to a team member. Not following up is a management gamble. It's possible that a team member successfully executed direction she was given, but it's also possible she did not. Without follow-up, the manager will never know or at least will not know until some negative consequence occurs because of the failure of the team member to execute.

Failure to follow up on an assignment or a performance standard is equivalent to a manager saying, "That is not important to me, and I don't really care whether you did it or not." That probably sounds like an extreme statement, and I do intend it to be extreme in order to make a critical point. If the manager doesn't want to take time to check up on an assignment, why should the employee invest serious time and energy in completing the assignment? I once heard a quote that makes this point in a very effective way. Unfortunately, the quote was not attributed to anybody in particular, so I can't give proper credit, but it goes like this:

> "The minute you fail to uphold a standard with good follow-up, that's the minute you set a new standard."

Some managers wonder why follow-up is necessary. It's understandable that managers would ask, "Why should I have to follow up? My employees shouldn't need babysitting. They should be responsible enough to do what they are asked to do." It would indeed be interesting if managers could simply communicate direction to the team and know that it will always get done perfectly and on time. Alas, that's not the real world. And thank goodness it's not because there wouldn't be a need for us managers. Corporate headquarters could simply issue direction by email and confidently trust it would be executed by dedicated employees on the front lines. But why is this not the case? I can think of four really good reasons for why follow-up is necessary and useful.

First, as we discussed earlier, team members all have different priorities in their lives, and 100 percent execution of company direction may not be at the top of everybody's priority list. That may be why they are not all in managerial roles themselves. It's not right for us to criticize where other people draw their lines in life. In fact, a certain part of me is envious of others who can happily live a more carefree life when it comes to job responsibilities. Rather than judge, I accept this reality and know that follow-up is my best tool to bridge the gap that divides us.

Second, follow-up gives us the chance to correct misunderstanding. Do you remember the example I used back in Chapter 3 about giving direction to the supervisor of the golf department for the order in which to place golf balls on a shelving end cap? I asked him to place a specific ball on the first shelf, and when I saw his completed work, he had put the ball on the bottom shelf. It was a simple misunderstanding. I was thinking "first shelf from the top," and he was thinking "first shelf from the bottom." It was nobody's fault. Well, okay, it was my fault for not being specific enough. But that's not the point here. If I had followed up soon after he started the project, I would have realized and corrected the misunderstanding long before he wasted all of his time doing the opposite of what I wanted.

Third, follow-up gives us the chance to recognize and reward successful execution. If a manager never checks back to see if an assignment was properly completed, that manager never actually sees it completed. Therefore, the manager can't give positive feedback to the team member who completed the task. Or, if she does give positive feedback, it will be hollow since it will be obvious to the team member that the manager never saw the end result. In this way, a very important reason for following up is to catch team members doing something right and then to praise them for their success. In fact, following up is a valuable management behavior even when a manager is 100 percent certain that a task was properly completed. As we learned in Chapter 4, appreciation and praise are highly efficient and powerful motivational tools, and quality follow-up is necessary in order to be able to give effective appreciation and praise.

Fourth, follow-up creates a culture of accountability. This is an incredibly important point, and I will use another story from my past to illustrate.

I was leading a foreign currency exchange company that had most of its "stores" in airport terminals. Our product was literally foreign currency, and our business depended on having the right amount of each currency at the right locations based on where flights were departing from. For example, if the flight to Stockholm, Sweden, was departing from Gate C-90, it was imperative that our store location nearest to Gate C-90 was fully stocked with Swedish krona (the official currency of Sweden). But, unlike typical retail businesses, the product, since it was money, was kept in locked drawers. Therefore, it was impossible to visually inspect from afar whether a store was properly stocked. In order to know if the right inventory was in place, the cashier had to run a special inventory report, called an F-10 report, on the computer, and that would generate a receipt showing the inventory of every currency that was in the till. I had been having a very difficult time getting the airport locations across the country to consistently execute the right currency/right place/right time standard. At least that was the case until I became relentless about my follow-up routine. I began using a five-step process each time I approached a store location in an airport. That process was as follows:

- Step 1: Say "Hi" to the sales associate working at the location.

- Step 2: Check the flight departure monitor to see the destinations of the flights departing from the adjacent gates.

- Step 3: Ask the sales associate for an F-10 inventory report.

- Step 4: Compare the departure destinations to the inventory shown on the F-10 report.

- Step 5: Immediately ask the sales associate and the manager to rectify any missing inventory for destinations departing from nearby gates.

I repeated these five steps over and over and over at every airport I visited. I was getting frustrated that I continued to find situations of missing inventory everywhere I went until something magical happened. As I walked up to the first of nine locations in one airport and did my Step 1, the sales associate interrupted my process by automatically handing me an F-10 report. I was flustered by being pushed into Step 3 before I had completed Step 2, but I nonetheless took the F-10 report from her, thanked her, and went to look at the flight monitor. Guess what? The location was properly stocked for every destination departing from nearby gates. My smile grew larger when I approached the second and third locations in the airport and the exact same thing happened. The airport manager had caught onto my routine and had begun doing the same thing himself a week before my visit. He knew he would be accountable for any inventory gaps, so he took the initiative and instilled the same sense of accountability in the sales associates at all of his locations. That same breakthrough was eventually achieved at most of our 250+ locations across the country, and it had an immediately positive impact on our business.

Follow-up creates a culture of accountability because it establishes expectations in the minds of team members. When team members expect the manager will follow up on a standard and will, if the standard is not met fully and properly, have it corrected and completed fully and properly, they realize it is easier to do things right the first time. When they expect the manager will not follow up, they may come to the conclusion that it is easier to not complete the standard fully and properly. In this way, failing to follow up on a standard sets a new standard that is lower than the manager's intention.

Frequency of Follow-up

Now that we have established the value and importance of follow-up, let's explore the idea of follow-up frequency. My comments thus far could be interpreted as recommending that managers follow up on every single performance standard and every single task assignment 100 percent of the time. We all know that's not possible. There are far too many things going on at any one time to expect that a manager can inspect everything. It's impossible for a retail manager to follow up on every customer interaction that her employees have during a given day, and that's just one of the many performance standards she must enforce with her team. So the manager must have a good sense for how to achieve a reasonable and effective follow-up frequency.

Unfortunately, like most things in management, it's a judgment thing, and there is not one formulaic answer. But I have identified three variables that managers can consider when they are deciding on follow-up frequency. One rule that cuts across all three variables is that follow-up frequency can (and should) vary depending on the task, the employee, and the situation. In other words, the ideal follow-up frequency with one task may be very different than the ideal frequency of follow-up on another task.

Variable 1—Follow-up Time Available
This may be obvious, but the number of things a manager can follow up on is partially dependent on the amount of time that the manager has available to use for following up. Following up is just one of a manager's responsibilities. We know from this book that a manager must also engage in behaviors associated with communicating, motivating, and growing talent (the other three management behaviors that are most closely tied to execution), and every manager has a lot of other stuff to do as well. Therefore, something less than 100 percent of her time can be dedicated to following up. With that said, remember from last chapter that follow-up can be a bridge to motivating, and we'll learn in the next chapter that it can also be a bridge to growing talent. That might make following up one of the most important activities a manager can spend time on. So managers are well served by dedicating as much of their time as possible to this highly leveraging behavior.

Managers often face the obstacle of administrative and/or individual contributor tasks stealing time away from managerial responsibilities. Sometimes these non-managerial tasks are necessary. For example, managers must take time to read their email, and, despite it being unavoidable, time spent reading email is time that cannot be used for follow-up on team members. Other times, managers get themselves involved in tasks that could be assigned to others. That also is time that cannot be used for follow-up, but in this case, it's a situation that is avoidable. Managers may find it more comfortable to take on tasks rather than spend time following up, and they may therefore rationalize that only they can adequately perform the tasks they are taking on. However, a manager's time is almost always more effective when spent on managerial behaviors like following up. The best managers find ways to allocate their time accordingly.

For more advice on time management, view my free video which you can find on my website at the following link: **http://www.RetailManagementFormula.com/time-management-workshop-for-retail-managers/**

This is an eighteen-minute video that could be a life-changing help for frontline managers who struggle with the daily challenge of controlling time. Not only does it help managers find time for follow-up, but it also guides managers through a process of creating structure for all of the tasks and routines they must complete in a day, week, or month.

Variable 2—Employee Skill Level
The second variable that should be considered when determining the ideal frequency for follow-up is the competence of team members. Highly competent individuals require less frequent follow-up than less competent individuals, especially when the purpose of the follow-up is to ensure proper execution and to correct possible misunderstandings. Readers are reminded, however, that another important purpose of follow-up is to catch team members doing something right, and to achieve that objective, managers must sometimes follow up even with the highly competent individuals. Managers who fail to follow up with certain team members risk becoming the "Hands-off Manager" from our Leadership Balance Model that we learned about last chapter, and that could lead to those highly competent individuals becoming detached and less engaged in executing their work completely and consistently.

When assessing the competence of team members, managers must keep two things in mind. First, competence is relevant only on a task-by-task or behavior-by-behavior basis. In other words, just because an employee is good at one behavior doesn't mean he is good at another. Beware of the halo effect where managers erroneously extend a positive assessment of some of an individual's skills to all of that person's skills. Second, competence is best assessed by personal observation or direct knowledge of a person's successful completion of the task or behavior in the past. In other words, a manager's most credible evidence of a team member's competence with a task or behavior is having personally seen the team member be previously successful with that task or behavior.

One thing that can impact the skill level of team members is the complexity of the situation in which they must execute. For example, a team member who possesses exceptional skill in servicing and selling to customers one at a time may struggle with doing so during exceptionally busy periods when multiple customers are demanding attention at the same time. Or a team member who works well on his own may face more challenges when working on a group project with other members of the team. When assessing employees' skill levels with a task or performance standard, managers must consider not only the technical ability for the assignment but also the ability to perform within the context of the environment and other relevant conditions that may impact the technical ability.

Variable 3—Importance of the Task or Behavior
The third variable to consider is the relative importance of the task or behavior. Items that are most important deserve the most follow-up time while items that are less important deserve less follow-up time. This is probably an obvious point since it's logical that more frequent follow-up will help ensure the most important items are executed most consistently. But it's also important because the frequency of follow-up itself communicates a message to team members about what's truly important. Employees will listen more to what a manager does than what she says.

For example, if a manager tells her team that customer service is the most important thing but then spends most of her time following up on operational tasks and little time following up on customer service, team members will learn to ignore her words and place more of their own priority on operational tasks. In other words, they will focus more on the execution of what her actions say is most important. For this reason, managers are wise to match the frequency of their follow-up with the relative importance they place on various tasks and performance standards.

I started the discussion of the three variables by saying there is no one formulaic answer that will guide managers to the exact follow-up frequency for every situation. After explaining the three variables, it may seem even more confusing. I am definitely not suggesting that managers devote a bunch of time to calculating how much follow-up they should do on various tasks. After all, every minute spent calculating follow-up time is a minute that can't be spent following up. The most important thing managers must do is carve out as much time as possible for follow-up. Experience will be the guide as to learning how much follow-up time should be devoted to various tasks. With the right mind-set, managers can learn to judge their allocation of follow-up time. That mind-set is as follows:

> "When my team members are not successful, it is my fault, and it's a sign I did not follow up early enough or often enough to help them achieve success."

This is a critically important difference from the typical management mind-set. Most managers, upon seeing a team member fall short of a standard, take the view that it is the team member's fault. Those managers get frustrated that they must "babysit" the staff or that they must "do everything themselves" if it is to be done right.

Under this mind-set, follow-up becomes a negative activity while under the mind-set I expressed above, follow-up is a positive, helpful activity. Not only does the positive mind-set motivate managers to devote more time to follow-up, but it also inherently effects the tone of voice that managers use when following up. And that has big implications on the effectiveness of follow-up. When the positive mind-set is in place and managers accept accountability for team members' failures, they internalize the lessons of insufficient follow-up frequency. Managers who truly feel responsible in this way begin to inherently adjust their follow-up frequency such that they are present at the right times to help team members achieve success.

Knowledge of the three variables I discussed in the last few pages serves as the subconscious framework for the lessons and the inherent adjustments. When faced with a situation where a team member fell short of an objective and the corresponding realization that his follow-up was inadequate, a positive mind-set manager reflects on the three variables.

- "Did I make enough time to follow up?"
- "Was this team member skilled enough to achieve success without more follow-up from me?"

- "How did this task rank on the list of important tasks that needed to get done?"

He files away the answers as lessons learned. In much the same way that repeatedly falling off of a bicycle leads to better balance over time, these lessons work together in his subconscious to guide future follow-up decisions. Again, it's all possible only with the right mind-set.

Feedback

An important component of follow-up is feedback, or communication, to the team member about what the manager discovered during the follow-up.

If the manager finds that the task or skill she is following up on was completed perfectly, the feedback to the team member is obviously positive. She wants to take advantage of the opportunity to reinforce the good behavior and thank the team member for successful achievement of the objective. If the manager finds that the task was not done completely or properly, the feedback is specific about what aspects were good and what aspects require further attention. She wants to be clear with the team member about what steps still need to be taken to successfully achieve the objective.

Feedback should occur as soon as possible after the follow-up is done. Immediate feedback makes positive reinforcement more effective because it is more closely tied to the time of the team member's performance. Immediate feedback also makes corrective action plans more effective for the same reason. The longer the delay in feedback from the time the employee performed a task, the greater the chance that other events occur in the meantime that will dull the memory and priority of the task that was the target of the follow-up.

When follow-up is done and feedback is not given, several bad things can happen. First, it's possible the employee who performed the task won't even know the follow-up occurred. If the team member doesn't know that the manager followed up, the follow-up can't contribute to the organization's culture of accountability, one of the key reasons for follow-up. Worse, the team member may come to the wrong conclusion that the manager doesn't care enough about the task to follow up, and that could lead to less commitment to the task in the future.

If the team member knows the manager followed up but he did not receive feedback, other negative consequences are possible. The team member may erroneously conclude that the manager was fully happy with the way the task was executed (a "no news is good news" story). That means that any aspect of the task that is incomplete or wrong will not get corrected. If the task really was executed properly and the team member receives no feedback, the team member might feel unappreciated despite having done a good job. And he or she would have a good reason for feeling that way.

One thing that should always be included in feedback is any coaching the manager sees fit to deliver to the team member. In other words, the manager should provide advice to the team member on what he might have done differently in order to execute the task with greater proficiency. Note that it's possible for a task to be completed fully and correctly yet there still be an opportunity for it to have been completed more proficiently. For example, a task may have been done properly, but the time spent on it may have been too long and inefficient. That would be an example of a situation where coaching would be appropriate even though the task was completed correctly. I'll cover the subject of coaching in more detail in the next chapter, so we won't get into it any deeper right now. In summary, feedback should accompany every instance of follow-up, and feedback should include the following three elements:

1. An assessment of whether the task was executed correctly or incorrectly;
2. If it was executed incorrectly, the steps that must be taken to correct it; and
3. Coaching for how the task could have been executed more proficiently.

Tips for Effective Follow-up

I'll now share some tips that can help managers become more effective with their follow-up. Employees expect their supervisors to follow up, and their personal feelings are involved. For example, people feel bad when their supervisor catches them falling short of a performance standard, and people feel resentful when they believe their supervisor doesn't trust them to satisfactorily complete a task. At the same time, follow-up must be accurate in identifying actual performance relative to standards, or the point of following up is lost. So to maximize long-term effectiveness, managers must consider both the adequacy of their follow-up and the feelings their follow-up evokes in team members. The tips below will help with that balance.

"Show Me, Don't Tell Me"
Managers often make the mistake of following up by asking team members if they successfully completed a task. The intention may be good. They want team members to feel trusted. In contrast, sometimes the motivation behind asking the employee instead of personally inspecting is managerial laziness. Either way, the problem is that team members may answer affirmatively even when the task was not successfully completed.

As mentioned above, team members feel bad when they are "caught" falling short of a standard, so they may tell a white lie or shade the truth to avoid potentially negative consequences. An example that happens countless times every day in typical retail environments is when a manager asks a sales associate if he helped a particular customer. The sales associate may respond, "Yes, I asked her if she needed any help, but she said she is just looking around and would let me know if she needed anything." Short of calling the sales associate a liar, there is little the manager can do but accept the answer. Even if the answer is technically true, there is no way for the manager to know whether the sales associate's approach to the customer was effective and in line with training the associate has been given.

In most cases, team members don't intentionally lie to their managers. Nonetheless, they may provide inaccurate answers to follow-up questions because they are mistaken or because they didn't understand the standard to begin with. For example, assume a shelf that originally contained a particular product is empty at the beginning of the day. The manager asks a team member to fill the shelf with inventory from the back stock area. The team member gets a handful of inventory and places it on the shelf. An hour later, the manager asks the team member if he filled up the shelf. The team member responds that he has. In reality, the manager expected the shelf to be filled with a whole cart load of inventory, much more than the handful that the team member used. By the time of the manager's "follow-up," the handful has already sold out, and the shelf is once again empty. Because of a difference in understanding, the manager thinks he has effectively followed up, and based on the team member's answer, he thinks the shelf is full when it is actually empty. At the same time, the employee thinks he satisfactorily fulfilled the manager's request and that he accurately answered the follow-up question.

There are other reasons why a team member's answer to a follow-up question might be inaccurate yet not an intentional lie. The team member's answer may have been accurate at one time, but conditions have since changed. Or the team member may be unwittingly relaying inaccurate information from another member of the team. You get the idea. The bottom line is that follow-up is not about catching employees in the act of misconduct. It's about checking to ensure standards are being met in a way that both manager and employee can agree on.

With all of that background laid, the most effective way for managers to follow up is to do so via personal inspection. Managers are best off seeing for themselves rather than accepting the word of a team member. "Show me, don't tell me" means managers should ask team members to physically show the product of their work rather than simply asking team members if the work was done. By physically seeing the results, managers are able to assess the results against the standards they had in mind. That will prevent miscommunication that will otherwise happen because of misunderstanding and mistakes.

Start with Trust

As I mentioned earlier, follow-up carries the risk of sending a message to team members that their manager does not trust them. That risk can be mitigated by the manager using language and tone that indicates a certain level of trust. For a basic framework for how to achieve this, refer back to Chapter 2 and the "Three P's of Positive Professional Relationships."

In addition to those basic ideas, I encourage managers to use some of the techniques that Dale Carnegie taught us in his bestselling book *How to Win Friends and Influence People*. (Carnegie, 1936) One Carnegie technique that works particularly well is his idea of giving the other person a chance to save face. A few examples could be as follows:

- "Will you please show me how much progress you've made so far on project *X*?"

The follow-up request contains an assumption that the task is not yet complete, so if the project is indeed not yet finished, the team member will feel less of a need to be defensive in her response. If progress turns out to be slower than the manager hoped, the manager can investigate the reason or reasons for the delay. Perhaps there are legitimate reasons that things are behind schedule, and the manager's role can be to help the team member get back on track. Or there may have been a misunderstanding on the timeframe or prioritization of the project. This approach gives the manager a chance to clear up the misunderstanding and get things back on track.

- "I know you have been juggling a lot of stuff today, so I'd like to do a check-in with you to see how well it's all going."

This follow-up request contains an acknowledgement that the workload is challenging, and it therefore makes it more comfortable for the team member to be cooperative in the process.

- "It looked like that was a challenging customer interaction. Please talk me through what happened."

This follow up request doesn't assign blame to the team member for bad handling of a customer situation. Instead, it implies that the customer may have been especially difficult. Again, this starts the follow-up process with an open mind to various possibilities rather than putting the team member on the defensive.

Follow Up in a Timely Manner
Just like my comments earlier concerning timeliness of feedback, follow-up should occur as soon after the start or completion of a task as possible. Notice that I said "start or completion." In many cases, it is appropriate for a manager to do the first follow-up on a task before the task is complete. That's the only way that follow-up can be used to identify and correct misunderstanding before a task is completed incorrectly. In any event, follow-up that occurs immediately is more effective than follow-up that occurs hours or days later.

Establish a Follow-up Plan in Advance
By establishing a specific follow-up plan in advance, managers can prevent the surprise nature of a follow-up request. That will reduce the chance of the team member feeling defensive during the follow-up process. It will also increase the probability that the team member will achieve success since it sets a tangible target for project completion and a tangible expectation for supervisor inspection of the result. This technique can take a number of forms depending on the skill level of the team member and the importance of the project. Examples include the following:

- "I'll come back to check in with you at 4:00 this afternoon."
- "When should I check back with you to see your progress?"
- "Please come back to show me how it's working out once you have completed the first three steps."

Introduce Yourself to Customers
This is a technique that's commonly used in the restaurant and banking industries, but it can work in any type of retail management environment. It is a particularly effective way to follow up on sales and service interactions that the manager did not have the opportunity to personally observe. It's common in restaurants for the manager to go around to tables, introduce herself to diners, and ask if everything is meeting expectations. Through this interaction, the manager can quickly get a sense for whether diners are happy with their experience, and it's a great way for the manager to get direct customer feedback on the quality of the food and service. A similar practice is used in retail banking. At the end of the process of opening up accounts for a new customer, a personal banker takes the customer profile to the branch manager. The manager reviews the accounts and services that were "sold" to the new customer. She then goes to introduce herself to the customer and asks a few clarifying questions about the profile. From this interaction, she can assess the quality of the job the personal banker did in determining the customer's needs and recommending bank products and services. In both cases, the restaurant and the bank, customers feel special with personalized attention from the manager, so the technique delivers a side benefit as well.

Because this practice gathers feedback directly from customers, it enables managers to see the true result of sales and service behaviors. Think back to the Behaviors–Results Grid in Chapter 1. We learned that there is a distinction between behaviors and results and that the two are not always the same. In other words, good results can sometimes be obtained despite bad behaviors and vice versa.

In the case of a restaurant, a server can deliver behaviors that are in line with company standards, yet the customer might perceive the server as giving bad service. This situation could exist because of a mismatch between company and customer standards, or the situation could exist because of some nuance in the delivery of the behaviors by the server. Either way, it is in the manager's best interest to understand the situation, either to discount that one particular result or to identify the nuanced behavior that must be corrected with the server.

The Empowerment Myth

I'll end this chapter with exploration of a topic that often comes up whenever management follow-up is discussed. That's the topic of micromanagement vs. empowerment. It is commonly argued by many self-professed leadership experts that an extreme amount of follow-up is a sign of micromanagement and that micromanagement is bad. They maintain that the best leaders empower their team members rather than micromanage them. By their description, micromanagement and empowerment are the extremes at opposite ends of a leadership continuum, with empowerment being the "good" end and micromanagement being the "bad" end. By empowering their people, these experts say, they enable them to grow from their mistakes and thus become more capable of performing well on their own. I never accepted the idea that lots of follow-up could be bad. I consistently found that when I relaxed my level of follow-up, I ended up with less predictable levels of execution from my team, and when I restored my relentless level of follow-up, team execution improved. I set about trying to resolve the discrepancy between my experience and the so-called experts' argument.

Bill Belichick is coach of the New England Patriots football team. Yes, the same Patriots team I wrote about in the prologue. While that story described (and, admittedly, celebrated) the Patriots' loss in Super Bowl LII, Belichick's record in his first twenty years as head coach at New England

(2000 through 2019 seasons) is incredible and includes the following accomplishments:

- Six Super Bowl Championships
- Nine AFC Conference Championships
- Sixteen playoff appearances
- Nineteen winning seasons
- 74.3 percent winning percentage

With these amazing results, and considering the experts' leadership theory described above, Belichick must be a tremendous practitioner of empowerment. And with superstars like quarterback Tom Brady on his team, he certainly has had the type of talent that can be empowered. In fact, Belichick does expect his players to make their own smart decisions during games. Yet everything I have read about Belichick describes him as a micromanager who is maniacal about attention to detail. He is well known for putting job candidates through eight, nine, and ten-hour interviews. He is well known for the agonizingly detailed review of game films he puts his team through each week. He is well known for issuing pop quizzes to his team members after these game film reviews. He is well known for relentlessly rehearsing every aspect of every play in practices. It sure sounds like Belichick uses micromanagement to prepare his team for success before he empowers them.

Let's look at a different kind of team. The United States Navy's SEALs are a special operations group that was originally founded in 1942 to do covert reconnaissance of landing beaches during World War II. The SEALs have become known as one of the most elite fighting forces in the world. A hallmark of a SEAL platoon is that officers and enlisted personnel train side by side, and each member of the team has a specific role and purpose. SEALs are empowered to make life-and-death decisions in the heat of operations, and each member of the team relies on decisions made by the others.

But SEAL teams are trained in an environment of unbelievable micromanagement. They endure more than a year of continuous training in every detail of their jobs, and they rehearse over and over and over again under the most extreme of watchful and critical eyes. SEAL training takes relentless follow-up to a whole different level, yet that is what enables team members to be successful when they are finally empowered to act on their own.

In the world of management, especially retail management, we don't have the benefit of a year of nonstop training or enough free time to do full-day video review sessions with the team. Much of our teams' preparation happens on the job. In order to set them up for maximum success, that on-the-job preparation must involve a certain level of micromanagement. Granted, the stakes are not as high as a Navy SEAL team operation or even the Super Bowl, but the principle is the same. It is not the case that micromanagement is good and empowerment is good. Micromanaged preparation enables successful empowerment. That makes micromanagement, i.e., relentless follow-up, good too.

While I do wholeheartedly endorse relentless follow-up as an effective and responsible way to prepare team members to be able to perform at their best, there are a few rules that go along with making extreme follow-up a positive experience for team members.

Avoid overly bureaucratic levels of follow-up. In other words, don't create follow-up just for the sake of follow-up or for the sake of management reporting. This sometimes takes the form of checklists and reports that employees must submit to management to prove they have done their job. These reports don't work. Good follow-up places the burden on managers; it doesn't create more work for the team.

Be respectful, and always maintain the self-esteem of team members. Even when follow-up reveals substandard performance from a team member, nothing positive is gained from berating the employee. Maintain a helpful, solution-oriented attitude even when correcting bad behavior.

Strive to catch team members doing something right, and seek to balance positive and negative feedback from follow-up. When employees know that management follow-up can result in a positive feeling, they will look forward to it rather than resent it.

Use follow-up to find opportunities to empower team members further. When follow-up shows consistently good performance, take it as a sign that team members are capable of contributing more. Expand employees' control and scope of decision-making accordingly, though also be ready to follow up on the expanded scope.

Manager Training Checklist #3—Following Up

These are behaviors or skills that managers should acquire in order to maximize team execution.

- ☐ Uses good time management practices to make an appropriate amount of time available for following up.
- ☐ Follows up on team members with an appropriate frequency based on their skill level and the importance of tasks.
- ☐ Maintains the proper follow-up mind-set that it is the manager's fault when team members are not successful.
- ☐ Gives feedback each time they follow up.
- ☐ Uses the "show me, don't tell me" method of following up.
- ☐ Begins follow-up interactions by establishing trust with team members.
- ☐ Follows up on tasks and behaviors in a timely manner as close to the point of execution as possible.
- ☐ Builds follow-up plans with team members in advance to set proper expectations.

Chapter 6: Grow Talent

Many years ago, I worked as a headquarters-based operations director for the factory outlet division of a national clothing retailer. Two of my responsibilities were to analyze business trends and identify ways to improve operational processes for the field team. Our structure included many district managers who each supervised eight to twelve stores, and those stores were spread out in remote areas that were not easy to travel to. As a result, district manager visits to the locations were less frequent than they were in more typical retail environments.

    I observed that store performance seemed to be better on the day of district manager visits than on days without a visit. It seemed logical to me; people are generally more on their toes when their boss is watching. I had access to the district manager visit schedules and to store sales data, so I did an analysis. I did indeed find that stores consistently performed better on the day of district manager visits than on other days. But the analysis yielded another important, and unexpected, lesson as well. For some district managers, the lift in performance lasted beyond the day of the visit. In some cases, the lift in sales lingered for a week or longer before settling back to a lower point. There was even evidence with some district managers that the lower point grew consistently over time. In other words, performance would spike on the visit day, remain elevated for some period of time, and then settle back to a point lower than the visit day but higher than the pre-visit performance level. For some district managers, this pattern occurred with many of their stores, and for other district managers, there was no lingering effect at all at any of their stores after the day of the visit.

    Intrigued by this revelation, I set out to learn why it was the case. I asked lots of questions, and I accompanied district managers on their visits. The answer soon became clear. District managers who produced lingering impact and ever-increasing baseline performance were doing so because they used their visits to teach. Conversely, district managers who produced a visit day spike in performance but no lingering effect used their visits to address in-the-moment urgencies and did not spend time teaching skills that could be used in the future. This wasn't a new idea. The theme has been around since at least the sixth century B.C. when the ancient Chinese philosopher Lao-Tzu, founder of Taoism, is said to have preached about the difference between giving a man a fish and teaching him how to fish. (Quote Investigator, 2015) But the visit analysis showed that there is a direct and positive business impact over time from teaching or growing team members' skills.

It's probably obvious that growing talent (i.e., increasing the skills and abilities of team members) is helpful to execution because more highly skilled employees are better equipped to meet standards and perform assigned tasks. But there are also a couple of more reasons why growing talent improves execution. As team members learn and grow, they become more engaged. We learned back in Chapter 4 that employees who are more highly engaged are more committed to consistent execution. Also, having team members who are able to perform more on their own means less management time is required to supervise them. That leaves managers free to spend more time on other things that drive execution such as following up on less capable employees. So growing talent is important to improving team execution in a number of ways.

I will spend the rest of this chapter talking about the three ways that managers grow talent. While there is some overlap among these talent-growing behaviors, they are separate, and each has its own purpose. The behaviors are train, coach, and review, and we'll now explore each in detail.

Train

The purpose of training is to give an employee new abilities or new skills. A new ability or new skill is one that the employee has not successfully performed on his own in the past. Under that definition, it would still be a new skill if the employee has previously been taught, has attempted it many times before, but has not yet accomplished it in a way that meets the standard. A team member is not considered "trained" on a skill until she has demonstrated that she can satisfactorily perform the skill. This is an important distinction. Managers sometimes make the mistake of believing an employee has been trained simply because that employee has been given information on how to perform a task. These managers consider their job done once they have told the employee how to do what they want her to do. Under that logic, we could expect sixteen-year-olds to know how to drive by simply giving them the drivers' manual and having them read it. There would be no need for learners' permits, mandatory practice times, and drivers' tests before issuing teenagers a driver's license. Admittedly, the stakes aren't as high with most tasks that managers assign on the job, but the concept is the same. Training is more than just giving information about how to do a task; it's everything that is necessary to enable employees to successfully perform the task.

A complete training process involves five steps. These five steps give managers their best chance to equip team members with the new skills they need to grow in their jobs. The process will work for any new skill, no matter how simple or complex.

Step 1—Communicate the Relevant Information

Yes, this first step is pretty obvious, and as I mentioned above, many managers make the mistake of thinking this is the only step involved in training. Communicating relevant information starts with telling the team member about the new skill they are to be trained on. That includes basic things like what the skill is, why it's important, what success looks like, and how to execute the skill. The more complex the new skill, the more detailed the information needs to be.

But even this initial step is more complicated than it seems on the surface. We know that misunderstanding often results from miscommunication, and misunderstanding in a training situation leads to unsuccessful transfer of skill. Miscommunication can arise for many reasons, including the fact that people have different listening and learning styles. So, in the process of relaying information about a new skill, managers must take every possible caution to prevent miscommunication. Some ways that managers can prevent miscommunication include the following actions:

Communicate all information in at least two different ways. For example, communicate by both email message and face-to-face conversation. Some people absorb written information better, and some absorb spoken word better. Most everybody gets more understanding from a message when they read it *and* hear it rather than just one or the other.

If information is being communicated in a group setting, like a meeting or a group email, follow up via one-on-one conversation with each member of the group. Some team members may pay less attention during group communication, and they may therefore miss important points without the individual follow-up.

Pass along information in a structured format such as clearly identifiable bullet points or use of sequential steps. Most people retain information best when it is broken down into small pieces, particularly if those pieces can be easily numbered or remembered. This is why acronyms and mnemonic devices work so well. It's easier to remember five clearly stated and bullet-pointed steps than a paragraph that contains the same information in a series of wordy sentences.

Include the "why's" for every "what" that is communicated. People retain information best when they can relate to the purpose. Sometimes the reason for a particular instruction helps team members understand exactly what the instruction is.

Enable two-way communication. Two-way means that team members can ask questions and provide feedback during the communication process. This is an important way to ensure proper understanding occurs. And it's not good enough to simply ask if there are any questions. Managers must create an environment wherein it is safe and comfortable for team members to ask questions. If employees feel like they will be negatively judged or impacted by asking questions, they will refrain from doing so, even at the expense of not fully understanding the instruction they are being given.

Ask team members to recite their understanding of the instruction in their own words. By having team members repeat the instruction themselves, a manager can quickly determine the extent to which they truly get it. If they say something wrong, the manager has a second chance to explain it before sending employees off to attempt the task.

Step 2—Gain Commitment
Just because a team member understands what a new task is and how to do it doesn't mean they are committed to learning or performing the new task. There are many possible reasons why an employee might lack commitment

to some new training they are receiving. Perhaps they believe it should really be somebody else's responsibility, they don't agree that the task is something the company should be doing, they don't feel they have the ability to perform the new skill, or the new training conflicts with some other training or responsibility they have received. These are just a few of the possible reasons. What's important is for the manager to recognize when there is a lack of buy-in to the new learning and then take action to gain commitment.

Managers can use the following techniques to assess team members' level of commitment to the idea of learning a new skill or task.

Ask them if they are committed. I know, another obvious statement. But I'm always amazed how often the most obvious solutions are overlooked. Usually, an open-ended question such as "How do you feel about learning this new skill?" works best because it doesn't allow the team member to shrug off the question with a simple "yes" or "no." Managers should take care to watch for contradictory messages in tone of voice or nonverbal cues. For example, the employee may say that she feels fine with the new skill, but her voice may hesitate, or she may avoid eye contact when responding. These are signs that the real feelings could be different from the way she answered.

Ask a less direct question such as "When do you want to get started with this?" or "How do you want to proceed with next steps on this?" The answers to these questions can be good indicators of team member commitment. Similarly to the last technique, managers should watch for signs in the tone of voice and the nonverbal cues.

If a team member admits they are not fully bought in to learning a new skill or task, the manager has a responsibility to find out why. As I mentioned above, there may be a very legitimate reason for the team member's lack of commitment, so further questions about the cause of low commitment must be asked without judgment and without causing fear of retribution.

If a team member says he is committed but otherwise signals he might not be, the manager has a responsibility to reconcile the difference. Directness is the best way to handle these situations. It can sound something like "I know you said you were on board with learning this new skill, but I'm sensing a little hesitation. What concerns do you have about it?"

There may be times when the manager must pull rank. For example, an employee may not be committed to a new task because he thinks it should be another employee's responsibility. The manager spends time trying to convince the employee that it really is within his job scope, but the employee fails to accept the point. There may be nothing left for the manager other than to tell the employee he is required to do it nonetheless. However, these situations should be few and far between. It is always best to find common ground, and that can usually be done through reasonable discussion. There can generally be some points of agreement such as "Yes, I agree this task is primarily Joe's responsibility. However, we need some other members of the team trained on it since Joe isn't here every day, and it still needs to get done in his absence."

Sometimes, gaining commitment to a new task or skill requires going back to Step 1 and explaining things again. Once the manager is convinced that a team member is committed to learning, she is ready to move on to the next step in the training process.

Step 3—Practice, Practice, Practice

Remember that a new skill is not "trained" until the team member is able to successfully perform it on his own. At the same time, a manager should not ask a team member to perform a new skill on his own until there is a reasonable expectation that he will be successful. The bridge between these seemingly circular statements is practice. Practice is the act of performing a task in a safe environment for the purpose of acquiring proficiency. Young children practice riding a bicycle with training wheels so as to be in a safe environment before they are capable of maintaining balance on two wheels. Sports teams practice their plays in a safe environment with their own team members before they are expected to perform in a real game situation. So it should be with employees on the job. They should have the chance to practice new skills in a safe environment before they face the pressure of using those skills with real customers or in live business situations.

For skills that involve customer interactions, role-playing is an effective form of practice. During role-play, another team member pretends she is a customer, and the learner practices the new skill on the pretend customer. The pretend customer can be a hypothetical example of a customer, or she can be a representation of an actual past or future customer. Either way, the learner is able to practice the skill without affecting a live customer situation.

A safe practice environment can be an actual live environment with a trainer present to oversee the action. For example, in the case of a new customer interaction skill, the learner could interact with a real live customer (rather than a pretend role-play customer), and a trainer could be close by to watch the interaction. In such a case, the trainer serves as a backstop for the learner, stepping in when things get too difficult or when the learner stumbles beyond recovery. This is regularly done in restaurants where a trainee server is accompanied by an accomplished server. The accomplished server makes sure that the trainee executes the process well and steps in when the trainee gets over his head.

The amount of practice required depends on the complexity of the skill being learned and the pace at which the team member learns it. Simple tasks or skills may require very little practice time while complex tasks or skills may require weeks or months of practice. Practice can be progressively more challenging as a learner gets closer and closer to being able to perform the new skill. For example, role-play scenarios can get harder over time, and then the learner can move on to supervised interaction with live customers. No matter the complexity of the skill, a team member should not be expected to perform a new skill on his own until practice demonstrates a high probability of success.

Step 4—Observe, Diagnose, Coach
This step goes hand-in-hand with Step 3. During practice, the manager or trainer must continuously observe the team member and assess how well she is learning the new skill. A main objective while observing is to identify points where the learner fails to meet the required standard. But it's not enough to just identify the failure. In order to be able to help the learner succeed, the manager must diagnose the reason for the failure. Only when the reason is understood can the manager provide advice and direction that will help the team member improve and achieve the standard. That advice and direction is called coaching, and I will talk about this in more detail in the next section. Suffice it to say in this section that the management tool that most drives the training process is coaching. Without effective

coaching, the first three steps are pointless. This is so important that coaching is its own talent-growing behavior.

Step 5—Inspect and Track Progress
This final step actually occurs after a team member has demonstrated readiness through successful practice. Its purpose is to confirm the employee is truly trained and to ensure that the training sticks over time.

Once a team member has received instruction on a new task or skill, the manager has confirmed commitment to the training, practice has occurred, and observation and coaching has led to a point where the team member is ready to perform on her own, it's time to take off the training wheels. The employee is given the green light to perform the new task or skill. The manager still has responsibility to inspect the team member's performance to ensure it meets required standards. The manager should continue to periodically inspect performance and track progress with the team member (note that this is a type of follow-up, so all of the aspects of that behavior that we covered in the last chapter apply here as well!). If the employee is able to execute successfully and is able to sustain success over multiple instances, the employee can be considered "trained."

This five-step training process might seem overly cumbersome. Indeed, for very simple tasks and skills, it probably is a bit much. But training of even the simplest tasks and skills can be unsuccessful, and when it is, the cause can inevitably be traced back to one of the five steps in this process. So even if the structured process was not initially used, the five steps can serve as a roadmap to resolving situations where training has somehow fallen short. If the five steps are consistently used, managers can be confident that their training efforts will result in growth of the talent on their teams.

Coach

As mentioned in the explanation of Step 4 of the training process, coaching is the act of giving advice and direction for the purpose of helping a person improve his or her competency with a skill or behavior. Note the subtle difference between this definition and the definition I provided for training in the last section. Whereas training is about growing talent through the addition of new abilities or skills, coaching is about improving competency with any skill or behavior. In other words, coaching can (and should) occur with new skills, already-trained skills, and even fully mastered skills.

Coaching is a natural complement to follow-up, the subject of Chapter 5. When a manager follows up, he does so with the goal of determining whether or not a task was completed to standard. If he finds that the task was not completed in accordance with the standard, he must give coaching to the team member. But, as I mentioned earlier, even if the standard was met, there may be appropriate coaching that the manager can give for how the team member could have completed the task with greater proficiency or improved efficiency. Since no two situations are exactly the same, there is always nuanced difference in the way a task is completed or in the results a particular behavior produces. This is the case for all members of the team, from least skilled to most skilled. That makes coaching a continuous necessity with all team members for managers who are truly devoted to growing talent.

Think about the big money world of blockbuster moviemaking. The biggest movies feature actors who earn tens of millions of dollars per film. Yet those superstars who have been perfecting their craft for decades still receive coaching from a director throughout the making of the movie. The director helps actors connect with the characters they portray and helps them find compelling chemistry with each other. Despite the fame and skill of the actors, the quality of the director can make or break a movie. Hence, the worldwide recognition of accomplished directors like Francis Ford Coppola, Steven Spielberg, Spike Lee, and Stanley Kubrick.

If the acting competency of Tom Hanks, Marlon Brando, and Meryl Streep can be improved by coaching from movie directors, then the competency of our team members for on-the-job behaviors can be improved by coaching from us as managers. Of course, it takes a highly skilled director to add value for the top actors. Similarly, it takes a highly skilled manager to grow talent through coaching, especially for employees who are already highly skilled at their positions. The following tips will help managers become the best coaches they can be.

Diagnose and Solve the Root Issues
Imagine you are the manager of a small retail store, and you see a sales associate greet a customer without a smile and with an unenthusiastic "Do you need help?" You have been very clear in the past in communicating

your standard that all customers are to be warmly welcomed with a smile and a genuine offer to help them with whatever they are shopping for. What's your first instinct? If you are like most retail managers, you feel the instant urge to reprimand the sales associate on the substandard greeting. And you will probably want to go straight over to the associate and reiterate your standard that all customers be greeted with a smile and genuine, friendly offer of help. The associate will reply with "Okay, sorry" or something similar, and you will beam with pride at your successful "coaching."

Except you didn't actually coach. You only treated the symptom. What you did is no different than a doctor who treats a wheezing, loose-chested cough with cough suppressant. The doctor didn't address the root cause of the cough, only the cough itself. The same is true with your handling of the unfriendly greeting. In order to treat the chest cough, the doctor must examine and diagnose the root cause, and so must you with the bad greeting. By reiterating the standard, you assumed the reason for noncompliance was that the sales associate didn't know or didn't remember the standard. That's possible, but it's unlikely since you were so confident that you had been very clear about it. There are a number of other possible root causes, including the following:

- The sales associate was in a bad mood because of something that happened in his personal life.
- The sales associate was in a bad mood because of something that happened at work.
- The sales associate had previously greeted the same customer properly, and the customer was rude in return.
- The sales associate had greeted the past fifteen customers in a way that was up to standard, and they were all rude in return.
- The sales associate was busy with an important task you had previously assigned, and the deadline for that task was fast approaching.
- The customer had just been properly greeted five seconds earlier by a different sales associate.

Do any of these explanations change the fact that the associate failed to meet the standard for greeting a customer? No. But does reiteration of the standard as if the associate forgot it address the root issue? No. By simply reiterating the standard, have you as a manager added any value to the associate's proficiency in consistently meeting the standard? Again, no.

Your job as the manager is to diagnose the root cause of the associate's failure to meet the standard and help the associate overcome that root issue. In order to do this, you must ask questions and carefully listen to identify clues. A good coaching conversation might start something like this: "I noticed you didn't greet that customer with a smile and a friendly offer to help. What's going on?" The associate may respond with an answer that immediately gets to the root issue, or it may take a series of follow up questions to get there. No matter how long it takes, it's not effective coaching until you get to the root and provide advice or direction to the associate on how to handle the issue in the future. If you determine that any of the six explanations above (or any other explanation) are at the root, you can address that specific underlying cause instead of addressing only the symptom. That gives you a better chance of fixing the problem for the future, and that's your main coaching objective.

Remain Patient
Coaching is a never-ending responsibility. Managers must sometimes coach the same behaviors and the same team members over and over again. It can get frustrating, and if it is being done often enough, it will almost certainly be frustrating at times. But, as frustrating as it may feel, it is important for a manager to always keep a patient tone when coaching. If the frustration comes through in the delivery to a team member, the coaching will feel disciplinary to the team member rather than helpful. That will have the opposite effect from what the manager wants out of a coaching conversation.

Of course there will be times when a conversation must be disciplinary rather than coaching. If a team member fails to change bad behavior despite multiple attempts at coaching, it may be time for a disciplinary conversation. Or if a team member falls egregiously short of a very important standard such as one that involves safety or security, it may be appropriate to have a disciplinary conversation at the first occurrence. In a disciplinary conversation, it is okay (and probably preferable) to use a stern, demanding tone of voice and language.

That said, most conversations will be coaching, not disciplinary. Managers should stay focused on the objective: help the team member improve his or her proficiency with a skill or ability. Helping is a positive activity, and it should be done with a positive tone of voice. So managers should coach with patience and keep hints of frustration out of the interaction.

Talk about Next Time
Coaching, by definition, comes after observation of a behavior that fell short of standard in some way. Accordingly, coaching conversations often dwell on criticism of the past behavior. While some acknowledgement of how the past behavior fell short is necessary, coaching will be more effective if the bulk of the conversation focuses on how performance can be better next time. Dwelling on past failure, on the other hand, focuses thoughts on the wrong behaviors and leads to negative feelings. So managers are more effective when they talk about "next time" in their coaching conversations, as in "Next time, try doing *X, Y,* and *Z.*" This satisfies the need to provide advice and direction and at the same time puts the advice and direction in a positive context. That technique is more likely to be encouraging to the team member, and it will be appropriately interpreted as helpful rather than criticizing.

Make the Fault Seem Easy to Correct
In Chapter 5, I referenced a technique from Dale Carnegie's book *How to Win Friends and Influence People.* Another tip from that book is relevant to coaching. Carnegie recommends that in order to change people without giving offense or arousing resentment, leaders should make the fault seem easy to correct. He uses a personal example from his past to illustrate the point. (Carnegie, 1936)

This is a technique that has always worked very well for me. In my experience, the highest value comes from the fact that it leaves the team member who is being coached with a feeling of encouragement and the desire to try again. A slight twist I like to use is to point out how the team member is now closer to the desired result than he was before the last attempt. Specifically, I point out how his proficiency has improved, and while it may still not be all of the way to standard, I compliment the forward progress. Of course I only do this when it's actually true, but there is almost always some degree of forward progress that can be identified. When team members feel like their efforts are making a difference, they tend to remain engaged and committed to moving forward.

GPS Coaching

We're all familiar with the way a GPS works to guide us to a destination. The GPS maps out a route and feeds us turn-by-turn instructions one at a time. When we miss a step or take a wrong turn, the GPS stops and goes into recalculating mode. It then issues new instruction to get us back on the proper route.

GPS coaching works in a very similar way. As a team member is practicing or performing a task or skill, the manager watches for the first sign of deviation from the proper route, or process. Instead of allowing the team member to try and complete the process, the manager intervenes immediately, points out the mistake, and redirects the team member onto the proper route. This prevents the team member from experiencing the additional trouble and frustration that will come from having gotten off track. After all, there is little to be gained from making the team member waste additional time and energy trying to find the way back to the proper route. More importantly, this approach keeps the learning focused on the initial mistake, and that is the important thing that needs to be coached.

This technique works very well in role-play practice situations and when it is combined with the technique of talking about next time. For example, during a sales role-play, imagine a team member forgets to ask the "customer" an important needs assessment question and begins to move on to recommending a product. The manager stops the role-play, points out the mistake, and instructs the team member to start over, this time remembering to ask the important question before skipping to the product recommendation. This is more effective and more efficient than letting the team member complete the role-play with an inappropriate product recommendation and then going back and trying to deconstruct where it went wrong.

Coach the Coaches

I'll wrap up my coaching tips with one that may be the most important. Coaching is a skill, and as such, it can be improved like any other behavior that might be coached on the job. An argument can be made that coaching is one of the most important skills that can be continuously improved because it is so complex and because it is so vital to the growth of talent throughout the team and the organization. Therefore, managers must always be looking to coach the coaches on their coaching skills. And that includes themselves. Managers must constantly evaluate the effectiveness of their own coaching, and when they fall short, they must give themselves honest, objective feedback on how they can improve their own skills. Yes, that's difficult, but if managers don't do it for themselves, who will? It takes a considerable amount of introspection, but it is worth the effort. Most importantly, it is consistent with the big idea that coaching is based on a genuine desire to help team members achieve success. All managers who truly believe that idea owe it to themselves to continuously make the effort to be better coaches.

Review

The third talent-growing behavior is review. This is similar to coaching in that it is a way to provide advice and direction that will increase proficiency, but it considers the big picture more than coaching does. Coaching focuses on a single skill or even a single incidence of the execution of a skill. Review is a broader and more comprehensive focus on overall job performance.

As we have covered at various points in this book, a manager who is dedicated to helping employees achieve successful execution will be spending a considerable amount of time following up, providing feedback, and coaching all members of the team. Each instance of follow up, feedback, and coaching is a data point. Some of the data points will be positive reinforcements of correctly completed tasks, some will be corrective feedback on tasks that were not executed properly, and some will be coaching advice designed to improve proficiency with a skill. If the manager is skillfully using the Leadership Balance Model that we discussed in Chapter 4, there will be lots and lots of data points in all three of these categories for every member of the team. It may be difficult for team members to make clear sense of so many data points, and they may therefore not be sure where they stand overall. Review is the way that managers pull all of the data points together into a single picture of an employee's performance. Specifically, a review conversation is one in which the individual data points are compiled and used to build up to an overall assessment of an employee's performance over time.

By definition, there should not be any surprises in a review conversation. An employee should never hear a data point in a review conversation that he or she has not previously heard as feedback. If that happens, it's a sign that follow-up occurred but feedback was, for some reason, not given at the time. Of course, it's possible that the feedback was given and the employee either didn't hear it or forgot about it. That's a different story. Also, it can be, and often is the case, that the review conversation is the first time for an employee to hear the overall assessment that was pulled together from a myriad of data points. After all, that's the purpose of the review conversation.

There are two types of review conversations: formal and informal. Formal reviews are the types of reviews that we are generally familiar with. They usually take the form of a year-end performance review where employees are given some grade or score, and their annual merit raise or bonus is tied into the process. I will talk about formal reviews in more detail later in this chapter. I'll start with informal reviews.

Informal Reviews

Informal reviews seem to be less common than formal ones primarily because they are not usually labeled as reviews. Actually, they are (or should be) considerably more frequent than formal reviews. Informal review conversations are those in which a manager communicates an overall assessment of performance, but the conversation takes place in an ad hoc way instead of as part of some formally scheduled process. Ideally, it happens whenever a manager has built up enough data points to form an overall assessment that she wants to communicate to a team member. Informal review conversations should occur frequently, and in that way, they become a type of continuous feedback that team members get used to expecting on a regular basis.

Informal reviews or continuous feedback might occur after the team member performs a certain task several times or when a team member is showing signs of having fallen into a quadrant on the Leadership Balance

Model other than the top right quadrant. Another common use of an informal review is as a status update or progress report toward agreed upon objectives. Finally, an informal review conversation might occur when a team member's overall performance is trending into unacceptable territory, and the manager wishes to intervene before things become unfixable.

Whatever the reason for an informal review conversation, one standard agenda can be used. It is as follows:

- State the purpose of the meeting/conversation
- Communicate the overall assessment
- State the individual data points that support the overall assessment
- Communicate next steps
- Communicate your role in helping the team member
- Provide closing comments

An informal review conversation to address overall performance that is trending into unacceptable territory might look something like this:

- State the purpose of the meeting/conversation

    "I want to talk to you to give you an update on what I have been seeing with regard to your performance with customers over the last couple of weeks."

- Communicate the overall assessment

    "I have a concern that you are not successfully balancing your operational responsibilities with your customer service responsibilities, and you don't seem to be responding to the coaching I have given you."

- State the individual data points that support the overall assessment

    "I spoke to you on the following occasions when I noticed you failing to provide proper service to customers who wanted help:

- Last Tuesday with the lady who had questions about a couple of products
- Saturday with the man who needed help with a return
- Yesterday with the family that needed direction on their best options

"And, I coached you three different times on how you could use pre-opening downtime to finish your operational tasks so those tasks would not affect the busy customer times."

- Communicate next steps

"I want you to take this seriously and make a change that will allow you to find the proper balance. Tomorrow, please get your operational tasks done before the store opens at 10:00, and then make sure you are 100 percent focused on serving customers when the doors open for business. If you are successful tomorrow, try the same thing for the rest of this week."

- Communicate your role in helping the team member

"I will check in with you at 9:15 tomorrow to make sure you are on track to get your operational stuff done by 10:00. If not, I'll help you make adjustments to get on track."

- Provide closing comments

"I know you have the skills to be great with customers, and knocking out those operational tasks early will make you successful. Thank you in advance for making a real effort to improve on this issue."

An informal review conversation to discuss a positive trend in performance and to reinforce the positive behaviors with a team member might look something like this:

- State the purpose of the meeting/conversation

  "I want to talk to you to give you an update on what I have been seeing with your level of customer service since we talked last week."

- Communicate the overall assessment

  "I am very happy with the progress you have made, and this past week you have delivered the level of customer service that is in line with our standards."

- State the individual data points that support the overall assessment

  "Each day that I talked to you at 9:15, you were on track, or we were able to work together to get you on track to get your operational tasks done before store opening. Then, once the store opened each day and you were fully focused on customers, you demonstrated the type of service skills that we both knew you possessed."

- Communicate next steps

  "This is exactly what I want to see from you, so continue doing what you are doing!"

- Communicate your role in helping the team member

  "Please let me know if you begin to run into problems again in the future with getting your operational tasks done before store opening. If that happens, I'll do my best to help you get back on track."

- Provide closing comments

  "Well done on making the changes necessary. I'm very proud of how you took on this challenge and conquered it."

Formal Reviews

Formal reviews are meant for a slightly different purpose. They typically serve as a documented record of an employee's performance relative to company standards. They usually cover a set period of time, often one year, and they usually cover a predetermined range of job responsibilities and performance objectives. Those responsibilities and objectives can be behavioral, statistical results, or a combination of both. And, as I mentioned before, formal reviews are often tied to decisions on annual salary increases and/or merit bonuses.

My assumption is that most readers of this book won't have the authority to create or change their company's formal review process. For those of you who do, I provide an ideal structure for you in Appendix I at the end of the book. For the rest of you, I have some suggestions below for how you can get the most out of whatever process your company has in place.

Establish a healthy routine of holding informal review conversations with all team members throughout the year. This will help you set them up for maximum success in the formal review process, and it will give you ample opportunity to discuss all aspects of performance so there are no surprises in the year-end conversation.

When reviewing statistical results, add appropriate context for behaviors. Remember the Behaviors–Results Grid from Chapter 1? The concepts behind that tool will add significant value to any formal review conversation about statistical results. Using this model will help managers put appropriate emphasis on obtaining results in the right way instead of rewarding employees during formal reviews for delivering results without regard for the use of desired behaviors. Managers lose credibility when they preach to their team about certain behaviors they want to see the team execute and then reward team members who deliver good results without following the rules the team is supposed to work by.

When you deliver your formal review to team members, use the same general format that I suggested in the previous section for informal review conversations. Specifically, communicate your overall assessment, then provide tangible data points that support that assessment, and end with discussion of next steps that will lead the team member to greater success in the coming year.

Approach formal reviews from the perspective that the employee's success or lack thereof is a statement on your success as a manager. If you view the main purpose of your role as helping the members of your team achieve success and they don't achieve success, it follows that you didn't achieve your purpose. Maintaining this perspective keeps your interests fully aligned with those of your team members, as they should be.

As I mentioned at the start of this section, if you are fortunate enough to have the chance to build your own formal review process, I have provided a structured program that will work very well. It's called the Annual Performance Planning Process, and you can find it in Appendix I at the end of the book. Even if you don't have the authority to build your own, read the appendix as you may find use for some of the concepts. A quick summary of the Annual Performance Planning Process is as follows:

Manager and employee meet at the start of the year to build performance objectives for the year. Performance objectives are a mix of objectives that cascade from company, department, and supervisor objectives, objectives that are uniquely written for the employee based on her/his role, and personal development objectives that are tailored specifically for the employee's professional growth.

Continuous feedback is used throughout the year to keep manager and employee aligned on progress toward the performance objectives. Continuous feedback is another term for the "informal review" conversations discussed earlier in this chapter.

A formal midyear checkup review is used to measure progress and address situations that may have an employee off track with regard to being able to meet annual performance objectives.

The process includes use of the start, stop, and continue feedback method to provide helpful coaching to employees. This method is a simple formula whereby the manager gives a team member one thing to start doing, one thing to stop doing, and one thing to continue doing.

<u>Growth Plans</u>

I remember when I was in third or fourth grade and we were given an at-home science project: grow marigolds. My mom took me to the store to get a packet of marigold seeds. I read the instructions, opened the seed packet, and began my assignment. The exact instructions are now a long-forgotten detail to me, but the instructions I recently read on a current packet of Burpee marigold seeds are as follows:

- Prepare the bed by turning the soil under to a depth of eight inches.
- Sow the seeds about six inches apart and cover with 1/4 inch of soil.
- Firm soil lightly and keep soil moist.
- Seedlings will emerge in seven to fourteen days.
- Water plants well during the growing season, especially during dry spells.
- Keep weeds under control during the growing season as weeds compete with plants for water.
- Protect plants from high winds and hot sunlight until they become established.
- After new growth appears, apply light fertilizer. Deadhead marigolds to keep them flowering.
- Monitor for pests and diseases.

What do you notice about these instructions? Two key things hit me. First, the instructions are steps that the gardener must perform, not the marigolds. Second, the instructions do not say, "Sprinkle seeds on the ground then walk away until they become beautiful flowers."

At too many companies, responsibility for employee development is placed on the employee. Yes, many companies have formal processes for individual development plans. They even have official acronyms for development plans, such as IDPs. But the IDPs are typically filled with things that employees must do to develop themselves, such as read a book, watch a video, attend a class, or complete some developmental project. Manager involvement is often limited to passing judgment on whether the employee is ready to be promoted or not.

In order to change the paradigm, I no longer use the term "development plan." I want to get away from the bad habits that managers have become used to from the typical employee development process. Instead, I use the term "growth plan" to reset the context in a way that puts managers in the role of gardeners. This way, managers become responsible for planting the seeds, watering the plants, keeping weeds under control, and applying fertilizer as needed.

The creation and implementation of growth plans is a side by side responsibility, with managers bearing the bulk of the responsibility for guiding the process. Yes, an employee has to be a willing and engaged participant. But the manager must lead by identifying the specific skills the employee must grow, finding the right activities to help the employee grow in the targeted skills, and using all of the management behaviors we have discussed in this book to ensure the growth process achieves success.

For some tools that you can use to guide your creation and tracking of growth plans, visit my website at

http://www.RetailManagementFormula.com/TRLPdownloads/

On my website, you will also find helpful tools for the process of finding, evaluating, and hiring top talent for your team. In addition, there are tools and links to free videos that provide additional support for many of the concepts we have covered in this book.

I have one final point about growth plans. It might seem logical to focus growth plans on improving skills and abilities that are deemed to be an employee's weakness. That logic holds up when a skill or ability is necessary for success on the job and the employee's competence is below some minimum standard. For example, if a job requires regular submission of written reports and the team member's writing skills prevent him from being able to submit an acceptable report, his writing skills must be improved. A growth plan focused on writing skills is entirely appropriate. However, if submission of written reports is a relatively minor part of the job and his skills meet at least a minimum threshold of acceptability, it may not make sense to devote a growth plan to improving his writing skills for a couple of reasons.

First, greater positive impact can probably be achieved with a growth plan that focuses on a skill that is more relevant to the larger job responsibilities. For example, consider a salesperson who must submit monthly reports. This team member spends all day every day selling, and he is required to write twelve reports per year. More benefit to the company and to the individual will be gained by growing the team member's selling skills than by improving writing skills.

Second, more benefit can be gained from focusing on an individual's strengths than on his or her weaknesses. A 2009 study by the Gallup organization found that 61 percent of employees who said their boss focuses on their strengths were actively engaged in their work. That compares to an average of 30 percent of all employees across the US who are actively engaged at work. One of the underlying explanations that Gallup found in this study was that workers who spend most of their day using their strengths are considerably less stressed than workers who spend large parts of their day focusing on their weaknesses. (Sorenson, 2009)

To some extent, we are all a product of our DNA. Add to that the fact that we are hard coded from a very early age with certain life experiences and environmental impacts. While I won't go so far as to say our personalities and abilities are unchangeable, we are certainly programmed with lots of talent in some areas and less talent in others. Our best selves are built by leveraging our top talents. The team member who has an innate ability to empathize, communicate verbally, and influence is better equipped for sales responsibilities than for writing operational reports. That person has a greater capacity to grow sales skills than report writing skills. The team member and the company will both be best served by a growth plan that focuses on improving his sales skills.

In conclusion, a solid combination of informal and formal review conversations will serve as a gyroscope for team members, helping them to adjust and realign themselves so they can remain on course and make continuous progress toward performance objectives. Along the way, they build skills that allow them to meet and exceed standards more proficiently. When used together, training, coaching, and reviewing allow a manager to grow the talent on the team. Talent growth keeps team members engaged, and it drives ever-increasing levels of execution.

Manager Training Checklist #4—Growing Talent

These are behaviors or skills that managers should acquire in order to maximize team execution.

- ☐ Effectively uses the five steps of the training process.
- ☐ When coaching, diagnoses and solves for root issues rather than symptoms.
- ☐ Maintains a patient and teaching tone when coaching.
- ☐ Talks about next time when coaching.
- ☐ When coaching, makes faults seem easy to correct and makes note of progress made.
- ☐ Effectively uses role-playing and GPS coaching during the role-playing.
- ☐ Coaches the coaches, including self.
- ☐ Uses frequent informal review conversations to create a culture of continuous feedback.
- ☐ Uses the six-point agenda to make informal reviews effective.
- ☐ Holds effective formal reviews that build from continuous feedback received through the period.
- ☐ Builds effective growth plans that focus on enhancing strengths and places majority of the responsibility on the manager.

Chapter 7: Building & Sustaining an Execution Culture

I started this book with a simple premise. The link between a good idea and good results is execution, and managers are responsible for driving execution. I then spent the next five chapters talking about the behaviors that effective managers use to drive consistent execution. When all is said and done, there are only two possible endings. Results will be either bad or good. Sure, there are degrees of bad and good, but there will be a line that separates results that are acceptable from those that are not. The first step to building and sustaining a culture that is based on execution is to make the most effective response to the results based on whether they are acceptable or unacceptable.

What to Do When Results are Unacceptable

In order to discuss a manager's ideal response when results are unacceptable, it's good to start by explaining what a manager should NOT do in that situation. A manager should not

- Wallow in self-pity;
- Wallow in self-doubt;
- Begin a quest to assign blame;
- Think up as many explanations (a.k.a. excuses) as possible; or
- Quickly change focus to new priorities.

None of those responses will produce a change in the results, and none of them will generate a productive solution to whatever problem exists.

There are three steps that a manager should take, and they must be taken in the order that I explain below.

Step 1 is to identify and fix any problem with execution. If this seems obvious, congratulations—you have paid good attention as you have read this book. Unfortunately, this often isn't the automatic reflex for managers. It is more common for managers to assume that execution was fine and instead jump to questions about the strategy itself. Further on this point, managers must look below the surface of what appears to be solid execution to identify the actual quality of execution. Sometimes people go through the motions of what they are supposed to do, but they don't actually execute with the thought and energy that is necessary to fulfill the spirit of the task.

    I have a great example from a point in my career when I was managing a market of consumer bank branches. We had been having a problem throughout the market (and the company, for that matter) with important communication not getting passed along to frontline employees, including tellers and personal bankers. The company came up with an idea: print out a daily "huddle" message that contained all of the important information the team needed to know, put it into a communication binder, and have every employee read and sign the huddle message sheet at the start of his or her shift. The concept seemed smart and easy to implement. In most of my branches, it worked, and I found that most team members were regularly informed on the important messages. But, in one branch in particular, I continued to come across examples of employees who didn't know about key messages that had been in recent huddles. I followed up with the branch manager to see if she was executing the binder and employee sign-off process. She said yes, all employees had been signing the daily huddle messages, yet the problem continued. I visited the branch and checked the huddle binder to see if it was in fact being used properly. Sure enough, the huddle messages were all in the binder, and the staff was indeed signing off on all of the messages. Still, the team seemed unaware. So I waited for an employee to start her shift. I watched from afar to see if she would go to the binder, read the huddle, and sign it. Sure enough, she did. Perplexed, I immediately went over to her and asked her to tell me what she had just read in the binder. She had no clue. Not even a general idea of the topic that was in the huddle message. I came to learn that employees in this branch were going through the motions of signing off in the binder, but they had such low levels of engagement in their jobs that they didn't even care enough to put in the minimal effort required to actually read the things they were signing. They knew they would get in trouble with the branch manager for not signing, but nobody was holding them accountable for actually reading and knowing the content.

In conclusion on this first step, if execution is the key link between a good idea and good results, it follows that execution should be the first point of inspection when results are bad. That takes real introspection because it's the manager's job to make sure his team is executing. When a manager's first reaction to bad results is to assume that execution must not have been good enough, it's equivalent to the manager assuming he did not do his job properly. That may be a tough pill to swallow, but it's the most responsible position a manager can take.

In order to verify if that assumption is correct, the manager must observe with maximum objectivity and lack of regard for his own self esteem. That means remaining open to learning the truth about execution—not just the motions of cursory execution, but the heart of genuine execution. And if there is a problem with execution, or the quality of execution, the manager must fix that before even thinking about moving on to any other possible solution.

Assuming execution problems have either been fixed or ruled out entirely and results are still not acceptable, it's time to move on the next step. Step 2 is to check on the details of the idea or the strategy. By this, I mean to assume that the big strategy is okay, but some smaller element or piece of it needs to be adjusted. I have another story from my past experience that can illustrate this point.

Back in Chapter 5, I talked about my days at a foreign currency exchange company. In that business, we had a constant challenge with finding ways to increase the average size of transactions (remember the ill-conceived incentive plan that drove wrong behaviors in the spirit of trying to increase average transaction value). I decided to try an idea that was fairly standard in some other types of retail businesses: product bundling. I gave the idea a name—Value Packs (I know, super creative)—and came up some "bundles" that would give customers extra value for their purchase if they bought higher amounts of foreign currency. Clearly not a new idea to most retailers, but it was a fresh concept in the foreign currency world. However, in the foreign currency business, there aren't many products to bundle. I threw in a prepaid phone card for purchases over a certain amount and a plastic wallet to hold foreign bills for purchases over a higher amount. I rolled it out with great fanfare, and I proudly told my boss about this new initiative.

Then I watched as it had absolutely zero impact on average transaction values. Our salespeople were trying to sell the new Value Packs, but customers just weren't biting. My boss all but said, "I told you so," and many of my own team members were up front with their opposition about continuing with Value Packs. While I accepted that something wasn't quite right, I wasn't ready to give up on the idea.

So we made changes. I asked lots of questions from the people who were on the front lines. I heard that customers didn't want the phone cards, and they didn't care at all about the plastic wallets. What they really wanted was a better deal on their foreign currency purchase. We changed the Value Packs to reduce service fees and improve the exchange rate for larger purchases. Finally, we started to see some small but consistent impact on average transaction values. We made a couple of more tweaks, including the addition of an opportunity to exchange leftover currency at the end of a trip at the wholesale cost with zero retail markup. We eventually found the right mix of offers and purchase thresholds, and Value Packs took off.

The concept ended up being adopted in the company's locations all across the world, and it was a reliable source of average transaction value growth for the next several years. If we had given up on the big concept at the early signs of bad results, we would have missed the huge upside that we ended up getting. It was only after we experimented with some of the strategy details that we found success. In addition, I learned an important leadership lesson. If I had engaged the frontline team in a meaningful way from the beginning, perhaps I would have avoided putting them through the unsuccessful trials of the initial Value Pack idea.

Now we come to Step 3. If you have ensured execution is happening consistently in a high-quality way and you have experimented with details of the strategy, and you are still getting results that are unacceptable, it's probably time to abandon the strategy. The best leaders know when it's time to give up on an idea and move on to something else. It seems like that would be an easy decision to make, but so many leaders have a tough time doing it.

Maybe they feel it's a sign of weakness to admit they were wrong, and that will cause their team members to lose confidence in them and their future ideas. In my experience, employees' respect for leaders who can admit their mistakes is much higher than it is for leaders who continue to push for their way despite clear evidence it isn't working. Maybe another reason for leaders to be reluctant in admitting failure of a strategy is that they have not yet thought of a better alternative. That's the perfect time to engage top team members in helping to come up with a solution. And even in the absence of an alternative, there is no point in wasting more energy and resources on an idea that doesn't work. Maybe their ego is so attached to the strategy and to the idea of success that they just can't accept the possibility of a failure. There's an old saying that if everything you do is successful, you aren't trying enough or being creative enough. Every idea or strategy will not work. The key for managers is to go through Steps 1 and 2 to rule out execution-related reasons for failure and then know when to accept the failure and move on to other ideas.

What to Do When Results Are Acceptable

When results are positive and it's clear the strategy is working as intended, the first thing to do is celebrate. But be sure to celebrate it as a team success, not a personal success. Celebration accomplishes a couple of things. It shows the team appreciation for the effort they put into executing the new strategy. Also, it reinforces the success and makes employees feel like they are part of a winning team. That increases engagement level and paves the way for smoother adoption of other new ideas in the future.

The second thing a manager should do with a strategy that is working is to ensure the success continues. It's one thing for the team's attention and energy to be focused on a new idea and for that focus to lead to good execution and positive results. But it's normal for attention, energy, and focus to wane over time as an idea loses its novelty. Eventually, the team will move on to other things, and the once new strategy will become yesterday's news. That's when execution levels can start to decline. The effective manager will carefully monitor for signs of this happening, and she will quickly restore the team's focus to bring execution back up to the level needed.

This can be a never-ending game of Whac-A-Mole, with managers constantly monitoring for declines in execution across a range of standards and quickly shifting focus to address those declines. That can get tiring and frustrating for manager and employees. The solution is to create a complete (and simple!) picture of all standards and to establish team routines that build habits around execution of all standards. Back in Chapter 3, I introduced the Management Pyramid. The pyramid is a tool that managers can use for exactly this purpose. It can be constantly updated to communicate all of the important standards that team members must execute, and the manager can use the pyramid to constantly monitor and evaluate team performance relative to those standards. It's a subtle difference, but rather than this being perceived by team members as shifting focus from one thing to the next, the team will perceive it as a constant focus on one thing—the pyramid—even if that one thing has many parts. By using the Management Pyramid to communicate all important team standards, managers are better equipped to maintain consistent execution of them all, including new and old standards.

The third thing managers should do when a new strategy is working is find more ways to leverage it for continued growth. In surfing competitions, the best waves are the ones that have the potential for the longest rides and therefore the highest speeds. The same holds true with management. Managers should ride the waves of success for as long as they can, and that will allow them to get the greatest results out of an idea or a strategy.

Remember the Value Pack story I told just a few paragraphs ago? After tweaking the details, we achieved success and got a year's worth of improvement in average transaction value out of the idea. As we came upon the anniversary of the beginning of the Value Pack success, we knew we would need something else new if we wanted to be able to take things up another notch in the second year. We could have looked for some other new idea to add to the mix, but we ultimately found a way to ride the Value Pack wave a bit further. Instead of reinventing the wheel, we did some simple tweaks to the existing strategy. We increased the value of the benefits to the customers and the Value Pack purchase thresholds. That small tweak gave us another full year of increase in average transaction value from the same strategy. We did Value Pack tweaks in each of the next several years, and we were able to ride the wave of this successful idea for many years in a row.

Creating an Execution Culture

The best way to ensure consistent team execution is for it to be embedded in a strong team culture. Dictionary.com defines culture as the behaviors and beliefs that are characteristic of a particular group. If a manager can get the entire team to strongly believe in the behaviors they are asked to exhibit, those behaviors become part of the team's culture, and consistent execution will be a product. Execution of those behaviors will be a natural part of the way the group works, and it will therefore require less supervisory "pressure" to make it happen. I have four tips for how managers can establish culture.

Create comprehensive execution plans. An execution plan is a proactive "road map" for how a particular task, behavior, or performance standard will be implemented with the team. It takes into account all four of the key management behaviors we have discussed in this book. This is important because it forces a manager to think in advance about all steps that will be necessary to help the team achieve complete and consistent execution. An execution plan can be used for a brand new task, behavior, or performance standard, or it can help with a revision to an existing task, behavior, or standard. It's not a complicated format, but it does require good thought. In fact, members of the team can be part of the process of building an execution plan, and that can help generate team buy-in to the plan. It's as simple as dividing a piece of paper or a whiteboard into four quadrants. Each quadrant gets one of four titles – Communicate, Motivate, Follow Up, and Grow Talent. Then the manager or the team lists in each quadrant the specific actions they will take in order to ensure successful execution.

Let's take a specific example. Imagine a manager has decided to make a change to the sales process her team has previously been trained to use. The change is an insertion of a step in the process that is designed to identify and overcome customer objections. The manager splits a blank piece of paper into quadrants, titles the quadrants, and lists relevant action steps in each quadrant. The resulting execution plan might look something like the chart in Figure 7.1 on the next page. By using the format of a four quadrant "Execution Plan" the manager ensures that she uses all of the key management behaviors to give herself the best chance of executing successfully on the objective.

Figure 7.1: Execution Plan Example

Objective: Add a new step to the sales process whereby team members must attempt to uncover customer objections and then overcome those objections to close the sale.

Communicate	Motivate
• Write up a document that describes what a customer objection is and how to overcome it. • Revise the documentation of the sales process so team members know exactly where the new step goes in the process • Hold a team meeting to explain the new step, why it is important, and what the new sales process standard will be. • Speak one-on-one with each team member to verify that they understand and buy into the objective.	• Find a different way to phrase "overcoming customer objections" so as to genuinely position it as doing a positive thing for customers. • Create a tracking chart to publicly recognize team members as they become "certified" on the new process. • Create a contest to reward team members who successfully identify and overcome customer objections most consistently.
Follow Up	**Grow Talent**
• Schedule specific blocks of time each day to observe team members with live customers. • Do at least three observations per day of each team member with a live customer and assess their success with identifying and overcoming objections.	• Rewrite the full sales process with the new step inserted. • Use role plays to practice identifying and overcoming objections with every team member until they can successfully demonstrate the skill. • Gather best practices from team members who are achieving the most success; coach other team members on the best practices.

Get the team out of ruts. This expression dates from at least the 1800s and refers to a wagon wheel getting stuck in a rut in the ground. Pioneers crossing the country for destinations in the west tended to follow the paths of those before them, and those paths were often marked by the tracks of wagon wheels in the dirt. With wagon after wagon following the same path, the ruts got deep. When a family or a group wanted to change direction, they had to lift their heavy wagons out of the ruts they had been in for many miles, and that was a very difficult task. So it is for a manager who wants to make a change with a team that has been in a rut for a long time. It takes extra effort to reverse existing behaviors than it does to create new behaviors. The team needs extra motivation to put in that extra effort, and it is the manager's responsibility to provide that motivation. The manager must paint a compelling vision of why the new direction will be better for the team and for the individuals on the team. When the team buys into the vision, it is more likely they will expend the extra effort to get out of the rut and move in the new direction.

Maximize reach times frequency. This is a concept from the world of advertising. Reach is the number of people an advertiser touches with a marketing message, and frequency is the number of times each of those people is touched. The goal of a marketing professional is to maximize reach and frequency or, when money is limited (and it always is!), to find the optimal balance of reach and frequency that delivers the most effective advertising result.

The same concept applies to a manager establishing culture in a team. The manager will want to reach all members of the team with the cultural message, and in order for the message to be most effective, the manager must maximize frequency of the message. The more times that team members hear, see, and read the message, the more it will be ingrained in their memory. The more it's ingrained in their memory, the greater the chance they will believe it and incorporate it in their behaviors. If the frequency is high enough for a long enough period of time, the team will eventually adopt it as part of their culture.

Create habits. In his bestselling book titled *The Power of Habit*, Charles Duhigg describes the scientific basis behind habits. He describes how a special part of the human brain, the basal ganglia, stores and retrieves habits as a way to conserve energy for the thinking part of the brain. Subjects who have experienced damage to their short-term memory are still able to perform habits that have been stored in their basal ganglia. In one incredible example, he describes a subject with short-term memory damage who couldn't remember where the kitchen was in his new house, but he could get up from his chair in the living room, go to the kitchen, and make himself a sandwich. That was possible because going to the kitchen to make a sandwich was a habit that was stored in a different part of his brain than the answer to the question of where the kitchen was in his house. (Duhigg, 2012)

This has enormous potential for managers. Managers who can turn execution of desired behaviors into habits for their teams have tremendous power to create a culture of execution around those behaviors. They do this by establishing routines that are so repetitive day after day that each team member's brain turns them into shortcuts and stores them in the basal ganglia as habits. Getting to this level requires use of other concepts we have talked about, including reach times frequency and relentless follow-up. But, once good habits are created, they are awfully hard to change.

Recipe for Cultural Change

Often, managers aren't tasked only with creating culture from scratch. They must also change an existing team culture. Cultural change takes even more work and commitment. It uses versions of many of the behaviors we have talked about throughout this book. My recipe for generating cultural change is as follows:

Step 1—Create a Compelling Cause
The cause must be something that every person on the team can identify with and can be motivated to get behind. You can use some combination (or all) of the following techniques to make the cause compelling:

- Identify a crisis that must be resolved.
- Ensure the "why" is clear and worthwhile.
- Rally a few champions who will incite others to get behind the cause.
- Create urgency via establishment of a critical deadline.
- Directly tie performance measurement to the cause.

Step 2—State a Simple, Memorable Vision
Structure of the vision should be a one-sentence statement of the high-level objective, and you can support the vision by two to four sub-objectives. The main vision must be an aspirational statement of the desired future. The sub-objectives must clearly tie to the main vision.

Step 3—Define the Process
Once the vision and the supporting objectives are established, you can define the details of the process to get there. The process must leave no detail to individual interpretation as people will tend to interpret based on the old norm rather than the new desired culture. You must carefully lay out the steps of the process in sequence as with GPS driving instructions. The clearer the process, the greater the likelihood of good implementation.

Step 4—Provide Relentless Follow-Up and Feedback
Cultural change involves the need to alter paradigms and move people out of established habits. This is harder than teaching a new skill from scratch since the journey is twice as long. Therefore, you must provide at least twice as much follow-up and feedback along the way. If the cause is truly worth fighting for, it is worth every bit of your time to ensure the team is pursuing it properly and executing it completely.

Step 5—Maximize Frequency and Reach of the Message
It is important for everybody on the team to understand the messages related to the cultural change, and it is important that everybody understands how important the cultural change is to you, the leader. Take every opportunity you can to repeat the message, and do so with as many people as you can. Use exactly the same words over and over again so that every team member knows them by heart. The message should become a team mantra. In order to get the team fully behind the mantra and prevent team members from rolling their eyes and shrugging off the repetitive message, tie the mantra to positive feedback that is related to the desired behavior change. When the mantra becomes a source of good feelings, team members will more readily adopt the message behind the mantra.

Leadership Integrity

The final topic I want to cover under this chapter's subject of building and sustaining an execution culture is an important and foundational message for this book. People willingly follow leaders who have integrity, and people resist following leaders who do not. They may temporarily or occasionally follow the direction of a leader they don't trust, but they do so out of fear. As soon as that leader isn't watching (and therefore can't apply consequences), people stop following. Establishing a culture of execution is infinitely easier for managers with leadership integrity. Leadership integrity is subjective, and there is no exact scorecard or set of rules upon which managers are judged. It's intuitive; employees feel it in a leader, or they do not. With that said, here are some tips for managers on the things they can do to increase the amount of leadership integrity their team members perceive in them.

Do what you say you will do. If circumstances change and you can't live up to a commitment you have made, tell the person or people you have made the commitment to as soon as you realize it, and let them know what you will be able to do instead.

Don't talk badly about people behind their backs. If you talk badly about one person behind his or her back, people will assume you'll do the same to them.

When you don't know the answer, say so. Don't guess just to look like you're in control. People will see through it, and they'll catch you when you're wrong. Admit you don't know, and commit to getting the answer by a certain time.

Give credit where and when it's due, and assume none yourself. Remember that it's the team that delivers the results, not you. You're just their helper. They deserve the credit.

Don't sugarcoat bad news. People want to hear the truth, and they are able to handle bad news, especially if there is a plan for how the bad news will be dealt with.

With that, I bring this book to a close. Execution is the amazing link between good ideas and great results. Managers are critical to driving execution. I set out to give managers clear guidance on the things they can do to drive good execution from their teams. The concepts in this book can also be used very effectively to troubleshoot situations of poor execution. What I mean by that is when team execution is either incomplete or inconsistent, the root cause can almost always be traced back to problems with communication, motivation, follow-up, growth of talent, or some combination of those four. The wise manager of managers or senior executive (i.e., one who has read this book!) will examine these four areas in order to assess the real cause of the poor execution and will aim to solve the execution problem by changing management behaviors. Even better, the wise manager will himself recognize problems with team execution, realize it is somehow his own fault, and switch into introspection mode to determine which of the four management behaviors he must improve. See Appendix III at the end of the book for a diagnostic tool that can help with this process. The reality is that execution problems emerge regularly, even under the best managers. The difference between the best managers and less effective ones is that the best managers recognize those situations and take personal accountability instead of blaming their team members.

There is an infinite list of responsibilities that fall on managers, but there is a handful of key management behaviors that are most directly tied to successful and consistent execution. As hard as it is to boil this entire book down to a short summary of recommendations, I'll give it a try. Here is my list of management keys to success for driving consistent team execution:

- Accept true responsibility for everything the team does or doesn't do.
- Be absolutely clear, urgent, and direct in communicating the standards you want your team to perform to.
- Be your own and your team's worst critic; be on continuous lookout for gaps between desired behaviors and results and actual behaviors and results.

- Devote sufficient time to personal follow-up of the team's performance, and have a sharp eye for identifying when and where performance falls short of desired standards.
- Manage to the spirit and intention of standards, and avoid creating administrative processes that miss the big idea.
- Ask enough questions to uncover and address root issues instead of treating symptoms.
- Balance critical feedback and pressure with positive feedback and confidence-building support whenever and wherever it is appropriate.
- Grow the talent within your team, and keep the cycle of higher talent and improved execution going continuously.

I would wish you good luck in your quest to achieve consistent and complete execution from your team, but it's not about luck. Though it's unlikely you will ever achieve perfect team execution, dedication to the principles in this book will get you as close as possible. Accept that it is your responsibility as a manager to help your team reach success, and you are well on your way to unlocking the power of the Amazing Link!

Manager Training Checklist #5—Building an Execution Culture

These are behaviors or skills that managers should acquire in order to maximize team execution.

- ☐ Follows the proper three steps in correct sequence when a strategy is not working as intended.
- ☐ Celebrates with the team when a strategy is working.
- ☐ Establishes systems to ensure strategies that are working continue working.
- ☐ Leverages working strategies to find ways for them to deliver continued growth.
- ☐ Uses the concept of reach times frequency to build culture within the team.
- ☐ Effectively builds team habits that facilitate ongoing execution.

Appendix I—Performance Planning Process

Note: The forms referenced in this appendix can be downloaded from the Retail Management Formula website at the following address: http://www.RetailManagementFormula.com/TAL-downloads/.

The objective of this process is to provide a vehicle for annual performance planning and assessment that does the following things:

- Gives team members the direction and guidance they want
- Cascades company and department objectives to all team members
- Involves team members in the setting of their performance objectives
- Connects each team member's performance assessment to the specific things that are most relevant to his or her role
- Complements and facilitates a process of continuous feedback

Annual performance management is a collaborative process between employee and manager that has four distinct stages. Progress and feedback are captured in two forms: the Annual Performance Planning worksheet and the Annual Performance Assessment worksheet. The stages and participants' roles are described in detail below.

Stage 1—Annual Performance Planning
The purpose of this stage is for employee and supervisor to agree on the specific objectives that will be used as measures of performance success for the upcoming year. The objectives can, and should, be a combination of business metric targets, project-related targets, and regular, on-the-job behavioral targets. The ideal process for building the objectives list is for employee and manager to each generate their own independent lists then meet to discuss and merge the lists. This format is meant to include the employee in the creation of her or his performance objectives, though the manager retains ultimate decision authority over the merged list. In certain situations (i.e., new employees, employees with recently expanded roles, employees in performance warning status, etc.), it may be more practical

for only the manager to generate the objectives list and communicate it to the employee. It is critical that the performance objectives be stated in as measurable a way as possible. This means inclusion of specific target metrics and target dates where relevant. The ideal list of performance objectives will include business objectives that cascade directly from company and supervisor objectives as well as one or two personal objectives that are aimed specifically at the employee's professional growth.

Next, employee and manager discuss and agree on the specific actions the employee must take in order to achieve the performance objectives. These actions can include routine behaviors to be carried out, new projects to be executed, changes to be made from past behaviors, etc. This is important because it bridges the gap from "what" must be accomplished to "how" it will be accomplished. Employee and manager also must discuss and agree on help or support that will be needed from others within the organization. This is important because it helps the employee to anticipate and plan for things that may get in the way of success in achieving the objectives.

Once manager and employee agree on all aspects of the performance objectives and they are well defined in a measurable way, the objectives are recorded in the appropriate columns of the Annual Performance Planning worksheet.

Stage 2—Continuous Feedback
The next important step in the annual performance management process is continuous feedback. The main goal of the process is to maximize employees' probability of success in achieving their performance objectives. To that end, managers and employees must meet regularly to discuss progress on annual objectives. Managers must provide feedback that will help employees maximize success, and employees and managers must have dialogue about obstacles that have the potential to derail success.

Stage 3—Midyear Performance Update
At a point near the middle of the annual cycle, manager and employee must meet for a midyear performance update. The purpose of this meeting is to formalize progress and feedback on the annual objectives for the year to date. Discussion during this meeting should center on the pace with which annual performance objectives are being met and the

effectiveness of employee actions thus far in achieving the objectives. Manager and employee should document progress and relevant notes in the top middle column of the Annual Performance Assessment worksheet. This will be very easy if continuous feedback has been in place throughout the half year. Progress and notes should carry forward from the continuous feedback meetings, and there should be no surprises during the midyear assessment performance update.

In addition to discussing and documenting progress toward the annual objectives, the manager should take this midyear opportunity to provide helpful feedback to the employee on behaviors. Specifically, the manager should highlight one specific behavior the employee should "start" doing, one behavior she or he should "stop" doing, and one behavior she or he should "continue" doing. This feedback is to be documented in the bottom portion of the Annual Performance Assessment worksheet in the columns titled "Midyear Comments."

Stage 4—Full Year Performance Assessment
This final stage of the process is identical to the midyear performance update, except it takes place at the end of the year and captures the full year of performance. The same steps are followed as in Stage 3, though it can be particularly effective to formerly note changes that have occurred since the midyear update. Assuming that all stages of the process have occurred effectively and the continuous feedback has been maintained throughout the year, the full year assessment will hopefully result in a celebration of success in the employee's achievement of the year's performance objectives.

Once this stage is complete, the cycle begins all over again. In fact, the full year performance assessment can coincide with the annual performance planning stage for the following year.

Appendix II—Summary of Management Behaviors That Drive Execution

Management Behaviors That Drive Execution	What the Behaviors Look Like in Practice
Communicate • General Information • Goals • Direction	• Use multiple types of messaging (verbal, written, etc.) • Filter communication (avoid too much) • Get to the point • Remain open and approachable (allow two-way communication) • Use the Management Pyramid • Set S.MA.R.T. goals • Use to-do lists • Create checklist routines • What, why, who, when, and how
Motivate	• Treat team members with respect • Give praise and appreciation o Participate in the task (when appropriate) • Use extrinsic rewards (carefully!) • Set challenging targets (not impossible targets!) • Appeal to a bigger team purpose • Take an interest in team members personally • Follow the Leadership Balance Model • Use the Tude-O-Meter to communicate about attitude

Follow Up	- Follow up with the proper amount of frequency - Maximize amount of time available for follow-up - Consider employee skill level with the task/behavior - Consider importance of the task/behavior - Provide effective feedback with each follow-up - "Show me, don't tell me" - Start with trust - Follow up in a timely manner - Build a follow-up plan in advance

Grow Talent	- Train—use the five steps
	    - Communicate relevant information
	    - Gain commitment
	    - Practice, practice, practice
	    - Observe, diagnose, coach
	    - Inspect and track progress
	- Coach skill improvement
	    - Diagnose and solve root issues
	    - Remain patient
	    - Talk about next time
	    - Make faults seem easy to correct
	    - Use GPS coaching
	    - Coach the coaches
	- Use informal reviews to connect dots
	- Use formal reviews as a record of performance
	- Build growth plans and play role of the "gardener"

Appendix III—Execution Problems Diagnostic Tool

Use this tool to troubleshoot situations of unsatisfactory team execution.

Assess Communication
- ☐ Do team members have an accurate understanding of the performance standards and/or direction they are to operate under?
- ☐ Do team members have the general information they need in order to succeed in their jobs?
- ☐ Do team members clearly understand the priorities?
- ☐ Is manager using best practices for effective communication (repeatable communication routines, multiple types of messaging, appropriately filtered messages, and open two-way communication)?
- ☐ Are performance objectives established in a way that is specific, measurable, assignable, realistic, and time-related?
- ☐ Are effective to-do lists and checklist routines being used?
- ☐ When direction is issued, does it answer the five key questions (what, why, who, when, and how)?

Assess Motivation
- ☐ Are team members sufficiently engaged in their work and in achieving the performance standards and direction?
- ☐ Does manager treat team members with respect?
- ☐ Do team members receive praise and appreciation when it is deserved, and is the praise specific?
- ☐ Does the manager appropriately participate in tasks without voluntarily "demoting" herself or himself?
- ☐ Are extrinsic rewards effectively in place in a way that is not driving unintended behaviors?
- ☐ Are challenging targets set for team members that are neither too easy nor too unattainable?
- ☐ Has the manager connected team members to a compelling, bigger purpose?
- ☐ Does manager take a genuine interest in team members as people?
- ☐ Do team members consistently feel both a high level of challenge and a high level of confidence on the job?

Assess Follow-up
- ☐ Are team members receiving appropriate levels of follow-up?
- ☐ Does manager dedicate enough time to following up?
- ☐ Does follow-up happen with enough frequency based on team member skill level and importance of the task or performance standard?
- ☐ Does a culture of accountability exist wherein team members expect that their performance will be followed up on?
- ☐ Does manager provide timely feedback to team members when following up?
- ☐ Does feedback include praise and/or coaching as appropriate?
- ☐ Does manager follow up via personal inspection?
- ☐ Does manager create follow-up plans in advance with team members?

Assess Talent Growth
- ☐ Are team members growing and acquiring the skills they need in order to be successful on the job?
- ☐ Are team members properly trained before being given responsibility to perform tasks or behaviors?
- ☐ Does manager use all five steps of the training process?
- ☐ When coaching, does manager diagnose and solve root issues rather than symptoms?
- ☐ Does manager remain patient when coaching?
- ☐ Does manager talk about next time when coaching?
- ☐ Does manager make faults seem easy to correct when coaching?
- ☐ Does manager use regular informal review conversations to connect the dots between multiple instances of feedback?
- ☐ When holding informal review conversations, does manager use the six-point standard agenda to make those conversations most effective?
- ☐ Does manager use formal reviews to establish collaboratively built performance objectives?
- ☐ Does manager create effective growth plans and take accountability for contributing actively to those growth plans?

Acknowledgments

I owe a big thank-you to so many people.

First, I want to thank the people I work with at Edison Properties. The owners and board members have been incredibly supportive of my desire to keep my writing efforts going while I have worked for them. And the strong team of leaders at Edison are an inspiration as they consistently demonstrate the behaviors and ideals that are so important to management success.

I have learned so much from the many, many great people I have had the chance to work with over the course of my career. That includes the bosses I have worked for, the peers I have worked alongside, and the wonderful teams I have been lucky enough to manage. You all were honest with me throughout the years about what worked and what didn't. That has been critical to my growth and success over the years.

Finally, but most importantly, thank you to my family. My wife, Tracy, has been my partner and my confidant for the last twenty years. In addition to being a source of good advice for me in my career and a proficient editor for this book, you keep me centered, and your perspective is always valuable, in life and in business. My sons Jake and Braden make me so proud and keep me motivated to continue to grow in my profession. I learn from you both every day, and I appreciate the encouragement you give me.

About the Author

Jon Dario has over thirty years of experience in managing a variety of different types of retail businesses. His background has spanned such businesses as hard-goods retailing, apparel retailing, retail banking, retail financial services, self-storage retail, and retail parking. Jon worked his way up from entry-level frontline retail management positions to district and regional-level management, headquarters leadership roles, and finally to the head position of several different retail organizations.

The Amazing Link is Jon's fourth book. Jon and his teams at many different companies have successfully applied the concepts in this book, and these ideas have consistently produced sustainable, positive results. After listening to the encouragement of others he worked with over the years, he decided several years ago to begin sharing his successful ideas. Jon's other books are *The Retail Management Formula*, *Management Is Not Rocket Science*, and *The Retail Leadership Profile*. Jon also has a number of online training videos that are available on various platforms and through his website.

Jon is the founder of the Retail Management Formula, LLC, an advisory company that provides consulting support for retail businesses. The company specializes in helping retail managers become more effective leaders. The company also provides sales training, business analysis, and other traditional retail advisory services.

To contact Jon about the book or his advisory services, email him at **Jon@RetailManagementFormula.com**, find him online at www.RetailManagementFormula.com, on Twitter @JonMDario, or on Facebook @RetailManagementFormula.

Audio Book Supplement and downloads of individual charts and forms in this book are available on the Retail Management Formula website at:

http://www.RetailManagementFormula.com/TAL-downloads/.

Resources

Alcorn, Randy. *Florence Chadwick and the Fog.* January 21, 2010

Apostolopoulos, Aris. *The 2019 Gamification at Work Survey.* TalentLMS. August 2019

Beck, Randall, Jim Harter. *Managers Account for 70% of Variance in Employee Engagement.* Business Journal. April 21, 2015

Bryant, Adam. *Google's Quest to Build a Better Boss.* Business Day. March 12, 2011

Carnegie, Dale. *How to Win Friends and Influence People.* Published by Pocket Books, a division of Simon and Schuster. Copyright 1936

Doran, George T. *There's a S.M.A.R.T Way to Write Management's Goals and Objectives.* Management Review. November 1981

Duhigg, Charles. *The Power of Habit.* Published by Random House Trade Paperbacks. Copyright 2012

Sorenson, Susan. *How Employee Strengths Make Your Company Stronger.* Gallup Workplace Business Journal. 2009

Garvin, David A. *How Google Sold Its Engineers on Management.* Harvard Business Review. December 2013

Quote Investigator. *Give a Man a Fish, and You Feed For a Day.* August 28, 2015

U.S. Census Bureau. *Employed Civilians by Occupation.* Statistical Abstract of the United States: 2004-2005

Vesty, Lauren. *Millennials Want Purpose Over Paychecks.* The Guardian. September 14, 2016

Made in the USA
Columbia, SC
09 March 2020